Everything Is Included

Everything Is Included

Essays About Truth,
Love, and Awareness

NIRMALA

Endless Satsang Foundation

www.endless-satsang.com

Cover photograph: © lekcej/iStockPhoto.com

ISBN: 978-1530731404

Copyright © 2016 by Nirmala

Note from the Author

This book is a collection of articles and essays. They cover many different topics that have come up often in the almost twenty years that, as a spiritual teacher and mentor, I have been sharing perspectives about our spiritual nature. Many of the essays have already appeared on my blog at http://endless-satsang.com/blog.htm, but I have collected them here for those who prefer to read a book instead of a blog. I have also included a few essays from my earlier books when it seemed appropriate, in addition to two appendices, "The Heart's Wisdom" and "Love Is for Giving," which are excerpts from my book *Living from the Heart*. These appendices contain perspectives that I have been sharing for years, and I recommend that anyone who is not already familiar with these earlier writings visit or revisit them to provide a foundation for what is shared in these pages.

May you find some truth in these words, and may that truth open your heart and set you free.

Nirmala, Sedona, AZ
March, 2016

Contents

Everything Is Included

The biggest spiritual truth is the truth of oneness. Everything that exists is part of a wholeness, a unified field that underlies reality. This is a radical concept because it seems to contradict our direct experience, where it appears that there are many different and separate things. Your body seems separate from my body, from the chair, and from everything else. And yet, two things can be very different without being separate. Your thumb is clearly different from your little finger, but are they separate? Or are they both also part of something bigger: your hand? Can't the same be said about any two parts of your body? They are different but not separate.

What about two things that seem so clearly separated in space, such as two bodies on different sides of the room? How can they be part of one thing when one can clearly see the space between them? While they are obviously not connected in the same way that two fingers on the same hand are, could they be connected in more subtle ways?

Right now, every object near you is affecting you. There are several different forms of energy flowing between you and every other nearby object, including light, heat, gravity, sound, and electricity. In addition, molecules are escaping from your body and the nearby objects, even solid inanimate objects. These molecules circulate in the space between you and every object and also land on and even enter your body. With every breath, you are breathing in some of the furniture and walls and other people in the room right now. In fact, in every breath is at least one atom that was also at one time inhaled by any other person you can name in history. There is even evidence that every single atom affects every other atom no matter how far apart they are. If that is the case, where does your body actually stop and the apparent other objects or bodies begin?

What about the space itself that you and other objects appear in? Where does space stop and your body begin? Is there still space where your body is located? As subatomic physics has shown, even physical objects are 99.9999% space, and the subatomic particles themselves are actually just clouds of probabilities. Are there really any boundaries in this infinite sea of space that we and everything else exist in?

All of this is pretty conceptual, and while it is all true, it still seems to contradict our direct experience, where for most practical purposes, you and I and everything else still seem so different that we also appear separate. Yet it is also true that fundamentally there is just one continuous field of energy, space, and matter in which we all exist. These are not contradictory truths but complementary truths. As mystics and lovers and true scientists have found throughout the ages, it is also possible to directly experience our oneness.

Without having to experience oneness with everything in this moment, can you at least experience a sense of connectedness or intimacy with something else or someone else? If you can taste the oneness you have with a lover or beloved pet or something that you find beautiful or inspiring, can you also sense a more subtle sense of connection with other objects or people? An even more profound way we are all connected is in our consciousness itself. There is really only one Being here, and we are all it!

What would it mean if underlying all of the apparent differences in our world, there is also an all-inclusive oneness? How would that change our view of our place in this world and our role in human life? Could it open our hearts and minds and allow a more kind, compassionate, and loving view of ourselves and everyone else? Oneness connects us all. We are all affecting each other in every moment, and recognizing this truth to whatever degree we can is transformative.

What if you treated everyone as a lover or a friend? What if you felt a bond with every living thing that transcended your individuality without denying or rejecting the infinite differences that also make up our world? Sometimes the perspective of oneness has been used to deny or reject other more relative truths, such as the existence of an individual self, but this makes no sense. A true understanding of oneness includes everything and leaves nothing out.

One of the reasons we resist the perspective of oneness is that we are attached to the more subtle forms of separation, such as the separation between right and wrong or true and false. We hold onto a subtle sense of separation to protect our sense of being right or our belief that something is true and something else is false. But what if, just as there is only one underlying reality, there is only truth? Many so-called opposites are really just different amounts of one thing: light and dark are just different amounts of light; heat and cold are just different amounts of heat; and wetness and dryness are just different amounts of water. Similarly, there are different amounts of truth.

Everything that exists is part of the truth, part of what is. This is not to deny that there can be extreme differences.

Bright daylight is profoundly different than a cloudy, moonless night in the desert. The wetness of the ocean is profoundly different than the dusty dryness during a drought. But they are all part of a spectrum. Truth is the same way. The biggest truth is the truth of oneness, and yet there are many smaller, relative truths that are still true, including the truth that your thumb is different from your little finger, and your body is different from everyone else's.

Just as there are extremes on these spectrums that are dangerous or even deadly (too little heat or water can kill you), there are truths that are so narrow and incomplete that they are tragically dangerous or hurtful. Just as we have a word for darkness, we have a word for truths that are that small: we call them lies or label them as false. The perspective that some things are false is useful for navigating the world, but it also remains true that every lie has some truth and reality to it. Some truths exist only as a thought in someone's mind, but a thought is still a kind of reality, just not much of a reality. A fictional story has some truth to it, but not much. Practically speaking, there can be so little truth in a thought as to be worthless or even dangerous if it is believed to be truer than it is.

Recognizing the bigger truth that all there is, is oneness or truth or light or love doesn't negate or eliminate the danger or potential damage of a more narrow truth. However, it does change our approach to the smaller truth: it puts it in perspective. If you think a small truth or a sense of separation is fundamentally bad or wrong, there is a tendency to reject it or even try to attack or destroy it. In contrast, if there is a recognition that everyone is part of one thing and everyone's truth is part of the bigger truth, then you would naturally approach other beings and other beliefs with more compassion and acceptance.

This doesn't mean you need to subject yourself to the hurtful or dangerous actions of someone holding a narrow perspective or someone holding a limited and prejudicial belief that incites violence. You can still protect yourself and others from those actions and any violence. Even the need to protect yourself is included in the whole truth. But in seeing the underlying oneness of everyone and every truth, you can also understand that the real cause of that danger and violence is the limited understanding, not some fundamentally wrong or evil nature that is opposite to the truth. The response this understanding naturally evokes in us can be imbued with compassion and clarity about what needs to be healed or made whole and more complete in ourselves and in others.

Oneness is not just a profound, underlying reality that we can experience for ourselves. It is a perspective that can transform the world and bring more love, light, compassion, and truth to the whole world. In every moment, we can notice how much oneness, how much truth, and how much love and compassion we are experiencing in ourselves or in another. If it is a lot, then what a gift life is giving us in that moment! If it is limited or contracted, then that is an opportunity to open our heart, our minds, and our awareness to discover what else is true in this moment. How separate am I really from the person in front of me? Is there anything about his or her perspective that can actually expand or enlighten my own? How can I possibly give some understanding, acceptance, or love and compassion in this moment in a way that can actually touch that person and bring more of an experience of our fundamental oneness and the bigger truth of the situation into this interaction?

Everything is included in this oneness that is pointed to by all spiritual teachers and leaders. In embracing everything with an attitude of its essential worth and value, we can sometimes go beyond the illusions of separation, right and wrong, and true and false to a simple resting in the beauty and mystery of all of reality.

What a Blessing It Is to Love What Is

Q: You talk about loving what is here, now. However, I have found I have become addicted to doing things I like and totally avoidant to doing things I don't like. I tried letting go of desire, but that hasn't worked because I still want the thing I am after. I am finding it really hard to love what is when I don't like it. I'm getting stuck and spinning in my head! I have not been able to let go of wanting a relationship, so the pain worsens. I am confused and wondering if you could shed some light.

A: Your confusion is natural and not uncommon. And yet, it is possible to love something you don't like. Certain things can make that easier to do:

First, remember that loving something you don't like doesn't in any way take away your ability to choose something different. If you don't like your job, you can look for another one. If you want a satisfying relationship, you can take actions to find someone and also to learn how to be healthier and happier in your relationships. Loving what is doesn't mean you become a doormat to unpleasant people or experiences or that you cannot move towards what you want in life. Loving what is just means that you don't need to suffer or experience a lack of love when you aren't getting what you want. It is part of life that sometimes we get what we want and sometimes we don't. So why not be filled with love even when you aren't getting what you want?

Second, it can help to simplify your definition of love to its most fundamental components. We may equate love with a feeling of attraction, affection, or appreciation, and yet the core of love is simply awareness and space. The simplest way to love something or someone is to give them lots of attention, curiosity, and awareness. Just touch them with your awareness and give them lots of space and acceptance. Giving space is simply a matter of recognizing that they are the way they are right now and letting them be that way. You don't have to like or feel good about the way they are, just be present to things as they are and let them be.

This is the essence of love, and it is the most satisfying way to be with the things you like and the things you don't like. You can give love in this way simply because it feels good to give spacious attention and acceptance to things, not because you want or need anything from them. You may still want something to be different or not like something, but in the meantime, why not allow yourself to be filled with a sense of fullness and love? Why wait for things to change to start giving this open attention to your experiences? It doesn't cost you anything, and you will never run out of awareness, so why not experiment with just giving love away freely? You may find you enjoy being curious and accepting for its own sake, even when you aren't getting what you want.

Last, but not least, the most helpful key to loving what is, is to include yourself in the equation, and especially to include your dislikes and dissatisfactions in this spacious awareness. If you don't like something, the easiest way to love what is, is to give attention and acceptance to the feeling of not liking it. That is part of what is, so why leave that out? If you don't like the feeling of not liking something, then start with giving space to not liking the feeling of not liking something!

When we start with loving our own feelings just the way they are, this can start the flow of loving acceptance and make it easier to go ahead and give space to the original thing that triggered our feelings. Even if you find that you can't give space to something you don't like, then at least you are experiencing some love and acceptance in the moment by loving how you don't like it.

The key to loving what is, is including yourself and your genuine feelings. By including more and more of what is already happening, experiencing and expressing more love becomes easier. In contrast, if you feel you have to get rid of your dislike for something before you can love it, then that just creates more internal conflict. That makes loving what is seem like a chore. But if you start by loving how much you don't like something, then there is no conflict; there is just some love beginning to happen. This can lead to loving the original experience, since it is easier to love something else once you have some momentum going.

One more thing about loving how much you don't like something is that most of the time you are already loving how much you dislike or hate something. When you are busy disliking something, you are usually already paying attention to how you feel and what you think, and you aren't trying to change the fact that you don't like it, so you are already accepting it. So the reason why this approach of including all of your likes and dislikes, feelings, reactions, and preferences can make it so much easier to love what is, is because your awareness is already flowing to these things. Before you think about it too much, there is even a de facto acceptance of your feelings. Awareness and acceptance are actually natural qualities of your Being that are always already here. It turns out this pure simplicity of love is not really something you do but who and what you really are.

The real gift of practicing giving love to people and things and also to your own feelings and reactions is when you notice that this acceptance is always already here. Loving is more natural and automatic to your Being than breathing. In every moment, you are loving (giving awareness and space) to something. By consciously giving this attention and curiosity to whatever happens to be here, you can begin to notice the constant flow of spacious attention that is at the core of your existence.

When we really start to sense how love and acceptance are always already here, then it may even seem like the problem is that our Being is too damn accepting and aware! Our Being accepts and is aware of everything, including all the ways we suffer and struggle. Yet, it is in the conscious recognition of this deeply unconditional love that is always here that the dilemma of our desires and suffering is finally resolved. If in a moment you truly sense the depth and completeness of this loving awareness of Being, then suddenly there is room for every thing and every feeling and everybody, including you.

For a long time, we think the way out of our suffering is to more effectively manage what happens. Then when we discover spiritual teachings, we decide instead to try to more effectively manage our desires. When none of that works, the only option left is to notice the place in our Being that already enjoys everything that happens, including all of our desires. At first, this can seem like an overwhelming defeat, but once you have lost all of your defenses, all that is left is this genuine spacious aware love. What a blessing — to be defeated completely by overwhelming love!

Apples to Oranges: Comparing Yourself to Others

Q: My mind loves to constantly compare myself to others, often in a negative way. I find that this mindset stalls my creativity and makes me feel downright sad. I also feel that if this keeps up, it will hurt my career, my life trajectory, and most importantly, my happiness. I have tried meditation, prayer, and seeking stillness in nature, but nothing makes this tendency go away. I know this is but one thought of millions and that all thoughts come and go. I know that I am worthy and that I am unique and like no other. Yet knowing all of this doesn't prevent the autopilot comparison mind from wreaking havoc inside me with all the negative emotions that come from this stuck pattern.

A: Our minds are designed to work in habitual patterns. This is a good thing much of the time, since that allows many of our actions to be unconscious. For example, we can drive a car without having to think about it. But when a habit is not actually serving us, then it is time for a new habit. I like how you refer to the autopilot nature of the mind. The mind is mostly a creature of habit, and once a habit gets going, it can have a lot of momentum. Most mental habits form because they were useful or seemed useful at the time. The problem is when a mental habit is no longer useful or not useful, like your habit of comparing yourself negatively to others.

The best way to deal with a habit that doesn't serve is to create a new habit to take its place. Trying to get rid of an old habit without replacing it with something else is like trying to not think of a pink elephant. The thought or habit is still the focus, and so it gets reinforced even by trying to get rid of it. Instead, I would suggest you focus on what you want to do instead with your mind and attention. Create some new habit and put your attention on it. A powerful question to consider is: "What do I want to do instead of comparing myself to others?"

There are three different levels from which this question can be answered. The first level is the level of the content of your thoughts. You can practice thinking about something else. You could even create some new comparing type thoughts, since that is what the mind does best. Just like you give a dog a bone so it won't chew on your shoes and furniture, you can give the mind a thought to chew on.

Often, a much more useful comparison is to compare yourself to yourself in the past. If you are considering your performance at your job, what happens when you compare how you are doing now with how well you did the first week at that job? Or how about when you compare your abilities now to your abilities when you first got out of high school? Or what about comparing your abilities now to when you were a child? These are more useful comparisons, since they illuminate the progress you have made. This is comparing apples to apples, while comparing yourself to others is more like comparing apples to oranges.

Another fun way to substitute a comparison is to make up ridiculous comparisons. What happens when you compare yourself to a cartoon character? Or to a mouse? Or to an inanimate object? By exaggerating how little use there is in comparing yourself to something else, it might become clearer that comparing yourself to other people is also pretty useless.

Another level of working with comparisons is to explore how true your thoughts actually are. The truth is what opens your heart and quiets the mind. Something that is less true will contract your heart and your awareness and make the mind even busier. Since some thoughts have a lot of truth and some thoughts have almost no truth, it can be much more useful to compare the relative truthfulness of your own thoughts. Your comparisons with others won't matter so much if you also recognize that those thoughts are not very true or important.

The third level you can explore is to make a habit of noticing what else is here besides your mind. If your mind is not serving you in the moment, try paying attention to your body instead. Or you can notice the world and the people around you. What if instead of paying attention to your thoughts *about* other people you paid attention to the people themselves?

This third level of exploration is endless. There are many dimensions and subtleties to the world and to the rest of your being besides your mind. Is awareness present right now? Is peace or love or joy present right now? What are awareness, peace, joy, and love like? How do you know they are or are not present?

Just focus on creating and doing the things you really want to do with your mind and your attention, and you will naturally spend less and less time comparing yourself to others without directly struggling against the tendency to compare yourself to others. You might as well spend your time doing what you really want to do.

If you find it difficult to carry out these suggestions, you might want to find a good therapist who is a skilled practitioner of NLP (Neuro-Linguistic Programming). One of the strengths of NLP is its ability to help people shift their behaviors. For example, one of the techniques in NLP is to imagine practicing a new habit in the future repeatedly in your mind. This is just as effective as actually doing it in the future and doesn't depend on remembering to do it in the future. In this way, you can create some momentum right now to the new habits so that they are as automatic as the old ones were.

Clearly this habit of comparing yourself to others is not serving you. What do you want to do instead? What new habits would you enjoy having? What else is here right now besides your comparing mind? There are endless possibilities of new habits you can create. What do you really want?

You Might as Well Enjoy Enjoying Yourself!

Q: I see everything as an illusion. We create our own reality. Everybody's movie is different from everyone else's. How can I stay motivated if everything is an illusion, and how can I change my reality in order to have other experiences in this play?

A: My favorite definition of illusion is that it is something real that appears to be something other than what it really is. The smoke and mirrors that a magician uses to create an illusion are real smoke and real mirrors.

So this illusion that appears as "you" and "your life" is not what it appears to be, but it is still real. Yes, it is a magic trick being done by the Being that you are, and yet the illusion is also made of that same Being. So the illusion is as real as the Being creating it. However, because Being is the doer of the trick, the place you find true motivation is in the Being behind the illusion.

This true motivation of Being is that it loves each and every one of its creations. That is its motivation. It creates because it loves to create, and it loves the creations/illusions it creates. If you can find that place in you that already loves your life and everything in it, that will also be the place where you find the motivation to keep going and the power to change what is happening.

However, that motivation might be very different than what you imagine it to be, because Being already loves everything just the way it is. So any change it creates will not come from a place of desire or unhappiness. It is creating and always will create from a place of total acceptance and curiosity. It doesn't change things to make them better; it changes them only to try something different and to have something new to experience and love. It loves and loves and loves, so every new experience or creation is a new opportunity to love.

What would you create purely out of the joy of creating? Even more importantly, what are you creating right now? What is happening right now? Whatever is happening is what you are creating right now, and that is what your Being is enjoying immensely. I often say Being is a total slut for experience—it will sleep with or embrace any and every experience that comes along. Find that indiscriminate love within yourself, and then find out how a conscious experience of that love likes to create. Being conscious of the creative joy of Being adds more depth and richness to the joy, but it is the same joy you have always had in the creation of this illusion called life. You might as well *enjoy* enjoying yourself!

There Is Never Too Much Love

Q: How can I detach from the love I feel for this person who has no interest in my loving him or in how I feel? I feel this beautiful feeling and, yet, so contracted that I have a heavy knot in my chest and abdominal area all the time along with a sense of extreme sadness. How can I liberate this love from this binding attachment? I feel like a compass that always points to the North Pole: my awareness always holds the thoughts of this one person and the feelings for him. Is there any way out?

A: Rather than detaching, I would invite you to attach more firmly to the *source* of your attachment. All attachments we have are only attached at one end: in our own heart. We never successfully attach to something or someone else. And so all of the intense and beautiful feelings you are having are coming from inside of you, not from the other person.

In a sense, the only problem with your compass is that you have been following the wrong arrow or pointer. The desire you feel points to the other person, but what about the other pointer on the other end of the compass needle? Where is that other arrow pointing? What if you follow your desire back to its source instead of out to its object? Then you don't need to detach or liberate or change anything about how you feel. All of the love and connection and intimacy you are seeking in someone else are already in the source of the intense desires you are feeling. You don't need to love him less; in fact, you can love him one hundred or one thousand times as much as you already do. Let yourself be overwhelmed by this love. Find out how much you can truly love by letting it flow completely.

In this process, you will be filled with immense love, and that is what your desire is really all about. We all have a deep innate drive to experience more love. The mistake we make is that we seek it outside ourselves. The source is and always has been inside of you. You don't really need a way out of loving him, just a way further into your own heart and the limitless love you find there.

Be gentle with yourself. Often the reason we don't allow ourselves to feel the complete depths of love is because, at first, moving towards the source of our love increases the sense of heartbreak and sadness. The relief from these overwhelming and painful feelings comes when we go even further into their source, but that can feel like leaping into the fire. The good news is that at the center of the fire, there are only flames and no more pain or heartbreak. So give yourself some compassion and tenderness along the way. But the final result is always worth it. There is never too much love, and so the only true antidote to your sadness is to love even more.

Love Is Both the Destination and the Guide

Q: I have fallen in love. I have not received much love from the person. There has been almost no communication and even less physical contact. When I met this person, it was a quick recognition that I was going to fall in love with him and that I already knew him from a deep soul connection. At first, I was so hurt when he pulled away from me, but I learned how to let go. When he is near me, I feel so alive. I radiate with joy and peace and love. When this person is gone, he is distant and hurtful. He pulls me in and pushes me out with equal force. But I remain patient and kind and loving. This person expresses to me that he has not learned how to love fully, but he loves me. So, how do I continue to love without overstepping my boundaries and while respecting his?

A: Love doesn't necessarily need a relationship. Love and relationship are both important and beautiful, but they operate at different levels of our Being.

Love is the bigger truth, and so it permeates all of our experience. The source of love is deep within our own essence. Even when you feel tremendous love when you are with the other person, that love is coming from within your own Being.

In contrast, relationship happens on the surface of our existence. For this reason, it is a smaller truth or reality. It is still important and worthwhile, but it is just not as important as love. A simple way to verify this is to reflect on how love without a relationship can still be wonderful, but a relationship without love is rarely very rewarding.

There is never a reason not to love. It doesn't cost you anything, and it fills your heart with sweetness and light. You can give love and then give even more, and you will never run out. To recognize this, it helps to remember that love is simply awareness and acceptance or space. The best lover is someone who gives you lots of attention and also the space to be however you are. You can always give this kind of love to yourself, to others, and to everything. Simply notice what is and let it be the way it is. You don't even have to like it, in which case you can also give space to your not liking it. (You can read more about giving love in this way in Appendix 2.)

When it comes to relationship, there are many more practical considerations. Is it realistic to be with this person? Does this person want to be in a relationship with you? Is he or she someone you can be best friends with? Does this person consistently treat you with respect and consideration? Is he or she able to listen to and accommodate your needs and also communicate and express his or her own needs? So it is simple to decide whether to love, but not as simple to decide whether to be in a relationship with someone.

When we confuse these different levels of our experience, we tend to suffer. When we forget that love comes from within our own heart, we may think we need the love of another person. When we deny or neglect our human needs to have healthy boundaries and nourishing relationships, we may hurt ourselves by pursuing or staying in unfulfilling relationships.

Often we are programmed or conditioned to seek a relationship with someone who is not willing or able to be in a relationship with us. To varying degrees, we all didn't get the love and attention we needed from our parents, and yet as a child, we still had to try and get their love. This can create a pattern where we feel compelled to get someone to love us even though they are not available for love. We are trying to get the experience we needed as a child by pursuing someone who reminds us of our parents, who were not completely available. These unconscious conditioned patterns have a lot of power to affect our relationships, especially if we are not aware of these patterns.

The antidote to our conditioned patterns and to the pain they can cause is, surprisingly, to simply love our own confusion and pain. Give your heart and all of its love and all of its wounding lots of attention and also the space to be here just the way it is. Don't leave yourself out when you give love freely to others. Being very aware of your own heart and its reactions will also allow you to become more discriminating about when and how to pursue or be in relationship with others. Love is both the destination and the guide in this life.

Truth Comes in All Different Sizes

Q: How do you know that our minds don't create all of our reality? Maybe there is nothing out there. Maybe when we die, we also become nothing.

A: The truth is what opens your heart and quiets your mind. Does holding the thought that there is nothing out there open your heart? Does holding the thought that when we die, we become nothing open your heart? Does it allow you to relax and just be? Or does it cause a contraction in your heart, in your Being? That is how you can determine for yourself how true that thought is for you in this moment. Checking in with your heart can reduce the need to figure things out with your head, especially when it comes to deep fundamental questions about our existence that cannot be known just by thinking about them. You can trust the knowing in your heart to sort out all of the ideas you encounter.

Everything we can think or say has some truth in it. But many thoughts are very small truths. They don't tell the whole story, and as a result, they could be considered a lie. It's helpful to be able to clearly discriminate when a thought is not very true, especially if it is such a small truth that it is harmful or deceptive. It is also helpful to be able to discriminate when something has a more profound depth of truth to it, such as a sense of the oneness of everything. While truth comes in all different sizes, it is possible to discriminate how true things are. A thought can be very true for you today and not so true tomorrow, as it is always relative to where you are in this moment. (Appendix 1 further explores how the heart can discriminate the relative truth of our ideas and experiences.)

Q: Spiritual teachers say, "Let everything be as it is." Then they talk about the world being in need of transformation. Is this a clue that they are all crazy, self-deluded, or fraudulent?

A: Another possibility is that spiritual teachers have a flexibility of consciousness that allows them to see things from many different perspectives and also to see different levels of truth that are true simultaneously. It is possible for two opposite things to both be true, either as complementary truths or as truths that operate on different levels of reality.

So it is possible to allow things to be just as they are and, at times, to also work to change or transform the world. These two perspectives complement each other. Most of our problems arise when we hold on too tightly to one perspective or the other. The real gift of any spiritual teaching is when it points us to the part of the truth that we are overlooking or ignoring. Most often, this is the truth that you can allow everything to be just as it is. But sometimes someone gets stuck in the view that everything is perfect, and they need to be pointed back to the possibility of changing the world for the better. As a Zen master once put it, "Everything is perfect, and there is always room for improvement!"

To Dive in or to Deconstruct the Ego?

Q: I would like to commit myself to awakening by deconstructing the ego and resting in awareness. This is pretty much what most nondual approaches suggest. But this is the wall I've come up against: the reason for doing so is to escape or transcend suffering. In other words, the nondual path reinforces the belief that what is happening now is not good enough. The suffering is evidence the ego/I notion is still operative, and so now I strive to achieve nondual oneness as a way to escape suffering.

An alternative approach might be to dive into the suffering and see where that leads. I've found such an approach fruitful but not liberating. It adds depth to my life and prevents me from being swept away by samsara, but it hasn't led to transcending it. So do I dive into the suffering or deconstruct the suffering by coming back to spacious awareness?

A: Your questions get to the heart of the dilemmas inherent in all spiritual paths and approaches. Practically, I suggest that you pursue both approaches. Sometimes dive into your suffering and other times deconstruct the ego by going directly to spacious awareness. The biggest freedom comes from a flexibility of consciousness and not from any particular state of identity or nonidentity. For the greatest degree of flexibility, both approaches can be helpful.

Ultimately though, you come up against a bigger dilemma, which is that there is nothing you can do to bring about a complete awakening or total freedom from suffering. Both approaches you mention are not capable of causing a profound release of over-identification or of your suffering, because both reinforce, to some degree, the idea that there is something wrong with what is happening, as you pointed out. When you dive into your feelings, it is because on some subtle level you are still trying to fix them or change them. And when you deconstruct the ego, you are also reinforcing your ego identity as the one who is deconstructing the ego!

However, even though the efforts you make are limited in their ability to cause a profound shift in suffering or disidentification from ego, these shifts still happen. The benefit of your efforts is simply that when one of these shifts happens, you are there to experience it. Understanding this can allow you to hold the results of your practices more lightly, since the results are not completely up to you. At the same time, it can help inspire you to give even more attention to the subtle workings of your inner spiritual life, not to fix it or change it or make something happen, but simply to be as present as possible to what is happening. What is really happening when you dive into the suffering? What is it like when you deconstruct the ego, both when it seems to be working and when it seems to be making things worse? Since these practices don't actually cause any profound shifts, the experience could be different every time you do one of the practices. What is really happening then when a shift does happen? Do you make it happen or does it happen to you?

The byproduct or side effect of all these approaches is that we are more present to our experience in the moment. This doesn't cause anything in particular to happen, but it does mean that we are "home" when a spiritual opening is happening.

Free Will Is a Part of Divine Will

Q: There is one big question that troubles me: As I see it, one cannot change or choose anything in one's life. To become free from all suffering, one has to learn to get curious and desire the complete truth at hand. To really live is to want this moment and this moment only. But doesn't this desiring also belong to the domain of free will?

If there is no free will, how can one really choose to focus on this moment and learn to love it? I think it is a matter of chance if someone learns to live and love in this moment and a matter of chance if one happens to read, understand, and implement the wisdom you present in your books. How can a creature with no free will choose to surrender to the Mystery? My view is that surrendering is not up to us: if it happens, it is a merciful coincidence. If this is true, then there will always be a group of people who can never be saved despite however good a spiritual teacher or psychotherapist is, who tries to help them. What is your point of view in this matter?

A: Your questions point to the mysterious dilemma of the dance between our true nature as infinite Being and our individual nature as a particular human being.

The biggest truth is that we do not choose, and it is the totality of Being that decides what will happen. And yet, within that biggest truth, there is also a relative truth, which is that we still do make choices. It is hard for the mind to hold these two seemingly opposite truths; however, they are not really opposite but complementary. Nevertheless, the bigger truth is that everything unfolds according to divine will. Our choices either cooperate with divine will or interfere with divine will, but only for a short time. Either way, the will of the Divine predominates.

It is my sense that this dance between our individual will and divine will is itself a part of divine will. Being is so complete and infinite that it can deeply enjoy the apparent difficulties and dramas created by its own creations. It loves seeing what we as individuals will do next, just as my wife and I love watching our dogs to see what predictable or surprising thing they will do next.

I agree that surrender and awakening are both movements of divine will, and so we do not choose surrender. Or it may be more correct to say that even when we do choose surrender, that alone is not enough to bring about a total surrender. Choosing to surrender is similar to how we may have a preference for today to be a sunny day, but we don't choose the weather.

However, choosing to surrender does have a more subtle effect: it means that we are paying attention to the movement of divine will. And this means that if by chance the Divine reveals more of the truth to us in the moment we are choosing to surrender to its impulses, we will be more likely to notice the bigger truth of our situation that is being shown to us. Surrender itself is not a prescription for something we need to do; it is more of a description of our true circumstances. Whether we are aware of it or not, we are surrendered to divine will. It is this bigger intelligence of Being that is making everything happen. But when we choose to surrender, we are more likely to notice the truth of our situation.

This is where our individual will has its greatest power: in directing our attention. When we direct our attention to the mystery of how little control we actually have, we are more likely to notice the Presence that is unfolding our life. We cannot change the direction of the Divine's will, but we can become more curious about its direction and its deeper nature.

As to your observation that there are some people that can never be saved no matter what they or a therapist or spiritual teacher does, this may only be true in a relative sense. Everyone is already saved as we are all already under the control of divine will. However, it is possible that this drama of the individual will dancing in opposition to this bigger truth can unfold over more than one lifetime, in which case we cannot say for certain that someone will never discover the true nature of their predicament. All the apparent individual expressions of eternal Being are also eternal. And eternity is a very long time! Will I be saved today, tomorrow, or a thousand years from now? Who can ever say for sure? But what a wonderful and dramatic story this dilemma creates. When we are the one living it, it is better than any TV show or movie ever made!

Q: Still, I am greatly perplexed. I understand that surrendering is to tune one's attention to see how beautifully the Divine reveals itself. Surrendering is not to choose the weather, but to choose to notice what the weather is like (and to be happy with it). But I still don't understand how I could freely:

1) control my motivation or preferences to look at the weather in the first place,

2) control my attention span and hold it onto current weather,

3) control my preferences to feel contented about the weather at hand.

I feel that attention and preferences are outside of free will.

A: It is easy to feel perplexed about this topic! Usually it means that we are holding one view or the other to be true, when both are true, and can even be true at the same time. Lots of opposite things can be true at the same time. You can feel happy and sad at the same time. You can want more ice cream and feel too full at the same time. And some apparently opposite things can be true simultaneously because they are true at different levels or from different perspectives. On a cloudy day, it is still sunny above the clouds.

Humor me for a moment and close your eyes and tap your forehead lightly a few times.

The "you" that just tapped your forehead is the same "you" that can choose to notice the weather or the flow of divine will. So from one level or perspective, it is true that you can choose.

However, at another level of truth or from another perspective this "you" doesn't really exist as a separate thing. So even when "you" choose, it is the larger field of Being that "you" are part of that chooses. From this perspective, the "you" that chooses is an illusion. An illusion is something real that appears to be something else. So in this case, the real Being that you are appears to be an illusion of a separate individual. And so from a higher or bigger perspective, this illusion cannot by itself choose anything because it is not very real, and when you are fully immersed in this perspective, it doesn't feel like you are choosing anything.

Both of these perspectives are true and correct. The confusion only appears if you want one to be true and the other one to be false. They are both true. However, this doesn't mean they are equal truths. The truth that Being chooses is a much bigger truth, but within that very big truth, the smaller truth is still true. Even the illusion of a separate individual has some truth, just not very much truth. All illusions are real, just not very real.

The only reason to understand this is so that you can hold both perspectives lightly. If you try to make one true and the other false, that is a prescription for confusion and suffering. If you think the only truth is that you are a separate individual and it is up to you to make everything happen the way you want it to, then you are going to suffer from that limited perspective and be confused and hurt when things don't turn out the way you want.

Since the bigger truth is that Being is doing it all, it is less obvious how holding that perspective rigidly can lead to suffering. And yet holding a bigger truth rigidly does lead to suffering and confusion. After all, how are you supposed to decide if it is not you deciding? Even if you just sit down and do nothing and simply wait for Being to do everything, you actually have to keep deciding to stay sitting over and over again, or you might get up by mistake and do something! If you hold even the bigger truth lightly, then it becomes obvious that you can just go on choosing to do things and not worry about sticking to the bigger truth. So in the case of what you pay attention to, pay attention to whatever seems truest in the moment to pay attention to. If that is the television, so be it. If that is the mystery of divine will, so be it. But "you" will still have to choose to turn on the television or leave it off, even though it is Being that really chooses.

Holding both perspectives lightly and even simultaneously means you can just go on choosing as needed. But also hold your choices lightly and even hold the results of your choices lightly, since not all of the choosing is happening through you. You can just relax and choose, and even enjoy the mysterious nature of choosing, and not worry too much about how it all turns out.

There is a story about a man falling overboard on a big ocean liner. The crew rushes to save him, and they throw him a life ring. The man tells them that God will save him and swims away from the life ring. Then they throw him a rope, and once more, he says that God will save him and swims away from the rope. Then they launch a lifeboat and start rowing towards him, but once more, he swims away from the boat, saying God will save him. Pretty soon, he is exhausted and drowns. When he gets to heaven, he confronts God and says, "I had total faith that you would save me. Why didn't you save me?" And God says, "What do you mean? I tried three times!"

That is the kind of thing that happens when you hold a big truth rigidly.

If you don't like the weather or anything else that the Divine is doing, the simplest thing to do is really notice your own preference. In other words, direct your attention to your preference, since that is what is happening, and so that also is the will of the Divine in that moment. What is it like to have a preference? How true does it feel? Does it open your heart and quiet your mind, or does it contract your heart and busy your mind? It is much easier to notice what is happening than it ever is to change it or to keep it the way it is. So the lazy way to choose is to choose to be curious and really be aware of what is happening. That is a small enough choice that the small truth of your free will has a pretty good chance of succeeding at it. You don't have to work so hard at it to succeed, and even when you don't succeed at simply noticing what is happening, you can always easily choose again to notice what is happening in this new moment.

There is another possibility. Sometimes we choose what Being is choosing. That is a very easy choice, and it can lead to an even clearer seeing of the illusion of free will. It just so happens that Being is very curious and very aware. So choosing to be curious about and aware of what is happening often turns out to be what Being is already doing. This can be a wonderful way to directly experience the bigger truth of the divine will that is here right now making all of your choices.

Your Consciousness Affects Everyone You Meet

Q: I feel I'm different than everyone I know somehow, and people seem to notice now too. I can't say how I appear different because I haven't asked, nor can I put it into words. I get both strong positive and strong negative reactions from people: they seem to either love me or want to run away from me. This wouldn't be a huge problem, but I'm finding that interviewing for jobs is a hit-or-miss with how people feel about me regardless of my qualifications. I am going on six months without any job in sight.

A: In regard to your question about the strong reactions to you that other people are having, I will share a perspective that I first encountered years ago in the book *The Lazy Man's Guide to Enlightenment*. Whenever two people interact, there are several possibilities. The first is that both people are equally open and expanded in their awareness. The second is that they are equally closed down and contracted in their awareness. In both cases, this is a comfortable situation, since the consciousnesses of both people are so similar. You may have heard the saying, "Misery loves company." This refers to the comfort and sense of support we feel when we are with someone with a similar degree of awareness. Being with someone who is in a similar state doesn't challenge or threaten our own state.

The third possibility is when one person is in a more expanded state than another person. We have all been on both sides of this, since our consciousness is always expanding and contracting from moment to moment and from day to day. When there is a difference or inequality in the degree of consciousness, it is still fairly comfortable for the person who is more expanded and open, since being comfortable with whatever is happening is part of the nature of expanded consciousness. However, for the person who is more contracted, being around an expanded, flowing, open-minded, and open-hearted person can be very uncomfortable. The greater awareness and loving presence of the more open person creates a kind of pressure within the person who is contracted. Someone's greater awareness seems to shine a light on another's contraction and limitation, making it even more uncomfortable to be contracted.

Ideally, this is an opportunity for the more contracted person to become aware of what is contracting him or her and to possibly let go of the limiting beliefs, feelings, or desires that are restricting his or her awareness. However, the first reaction of the more contracted person is often to try to get the more expanded person to contract. This makes some sense because if he or she is successful at getting the other person to contract, the consciousness will be more equal and therefore more comfortable. So those who are more contracted will often criticize, tease, confront, or even attack those who are more expanded. Or they might shower them with excessive praise and compliments, as that can also make someone contract into a limited identity.

It can be helpful for the person who is more expanded to consciously recognize that this is what is happening. If there seems to be a possibility that the other person will give up his or her attempt to get you to contract, and you are willing to stay in the situation until that happens, this can be a wonderful opportunity to help someone experience his or her own capacity for greater awareness and love. However, you are under no obligation to stay around someone who is actively trying to undermine your consciousness. It doesn't serve anyone to stay in such a situation. You are always free to move away or leave any situation, especially if this pattern is not part of an ongoing relationship.

This dynamic is just one part of the rich interplay of human interactions. Obviously, it becomes much more complicated when there are more than two people, or when there is a longer term relationship involved and other aspects of our conditioning are being triggered, or when other factors are also involved, such as when the difficult relationship is just one small part of a bigger situation, such as a job or your family. In the case of a longer term relationship, the question becomes, What is the overall climate or reality of the relationship? If someone else is trying to get you to contract in this moment, but overall there is a lot of love, acceptance, and openness within the relationship, it becomes more worthwhile to stay until the current difficulty passes.

As for the specific challenge of finding a job, being aware of this overall dynamic may allow you to meet someone where he or she is at. If you consciously choose to contract your awareness to make the interviewer more comfortable, that isn't a problem. You may not want to or even need to join him or her in any overt negativity, but you might be able to focus your attention in that moment on the very practical matters at hand regarding the job itself, which can be a relative contraction of your awareness. If this is your choice to, in a sense, be more normal in that moment, then it might be okay to temporarily join that person wherever he or she is.

The good news is that when our consciousness contracts, either by choice or when we are triggered, there is no harm done. Consciousness is infinitely flexible and can always return to its original shape. The ultimate freedom is not necessarily to always be expanded, but to have the flexibility to move into whatever state of consciousness serves in each moment. You might become curious during your interviews and simply experiment with different states of consciousness to see if you can discover the one that fits best with the specific person you are encountering, especially if you sense that the job in question would overall be a good fit for you. Sometimes this will happen spontaneously. As you mentioned, sometimes people respond very positively to you. But if there is clearly a discomfort in the other person that you can address without really sacrificing your integrity, then it might be possible to meet him or her somewhere in the middle.

Your consciousness will affect everyone you meet even if you don't interact with them directly, and it will affect them even more if you do interact with them. It is not your fault or even your responsibility if someone is uncomfortable in your presence. And yet when you do meet someone who can join you where you already are in consciousness, what a blessing that is!

How Sweet Air Is After We Go Without It for a While!

Q: Why does our consciousness continuously fluctuate between an expanded state and a contracted state? Why can't we perpetually remain in an expanded state of consciousness and feel at peace all the time? How can we attain that state?

A: Consciousness seems to like to experience all states and all possibilities. So as wonderful and beautiful as expanded states of peace and bliss are, life seems to want to try it every which way. In part, this is because the contrast between expansion and contraction is what allows us to appreciate the expansion when it happens. If we were eternally, infinitely expanded, we would hardly know it, since it would be so constant, just as we rarely notice the air we breathe because it is constantly present. But when we go for a moment or two without air, we suddenly really appreciate breathing again!

There is an even bigger freedom than being constantly expanded, and that is to have had enough experiences of expansion that it simply doesn't matter anymore if you are experiencing it right now or not. The flexibility to expand and contract allows our Being to respond in whatever way is most appropriate to the moment. Sometimes the truest response is to contract or focus our awareness, like when we are eating chocolate. It would be a waste of good chocolate to be in cosmic consciousness while we are eating it!

As for how to attain those expanded states, the state you experience isn't completely up to you. However, you can pay attention and be curious about your state so that you experience it fully. This applies to the ordinary states and the most expanded states. The real purpose of spiritual techniques, including meditation, inquiry, satsang, and mindfulness is not to cause shifts in your consciousness, but to engage you with your consciousness so that you are aware of the shifts when they do happen.

The Purpose of Life

Q: Is there any purpose to it all?

A: There are several possibilities, and you get to choose which one is true for you. You can see life as pointless, and it will feel pointless to you, or you can decide it has a purpose. You can even decide what the purpose is, and for you that will be the purpose.

But, even simpler, is to let everything be its own purpose. So when you go for a walk, the purpose is to go for a walk. When you pick a career, the purpose is to pick a career. When you decide not to choose a career, the purpose is to experience not choosing a career.

It is much more complicated when the purpose is something other than the thing itself. For instance, if you go for a walk to lose weight or get fit, the purpose of the walk has become much more complicated. Or if you choose a career to make your parents happy or to make yourself happy, then there is more at stake than just the choice of a career, which usually doesn't make anyone happy or unhappy. Most people choose to be happy or choose to be unhappy, and so career choices that you or others make are just an excuse to go ahead and make the choice to be happy or unhappy. Things are simpler if you just choose to be happy for the purpose of being happy!

From this simpler perspective, life doesn't have to get anywhere in particular, because wherever you are and wherever you are going is also the purpose in this moment. The journey *is* the destination. Even if the experiences turn out to be random, then the purpose is to experience randomness!

Joy and Gratitude for Not Eating a Cookie!

Q: I listened to your interview on "Buddha at the Gas Pump," and I disagree with the idea that decadence and indulgence are something to avoid. Even eating sweets and feeling bad seems to be just another experience, a particular kind of experience, with lots of discomfort and self-recrimination, but essentially just another experience.

A: I hear you that indulgence and decadence are just different experiences. Consciousness cannot be harmed, so it is willing to try anything and everything! And there is a natural wisdom and discrimination that can develop also. William Blake once said, "The path of excess leads to the palace of Wisdom." This suggests there is a place of Wisdom where the whole truth of excess and indulgence is seen, and a different choice can be made, not from a place of recrimination or judgment, but simply from a place of choosing something different.

When I stopped indulging in sweets it was not from a place of feeling bad about myself or even about sweets. It was simply a seeing of the whole truth of how sugary foods felt and making a choice to feel differently. There was no struggle or sense of denial to it, and I still occasionally make the choice to indulge, just much less than before when there seemed to be no choice. If I saw a cookie, I ate it! Now I look at a cookie and I can imagine both how it will feel in my mouth and how my body will feel in half an hour. When I include the whole truth of the cookie, it is rarely worth the fleeting pleasure it gives. However, if a dear friend has baked a batch of cookies just for me, then the whole truth will probably mean eating a few with a sense of joy and gratitude. But most of the time, I feel a sense of joy and gratitude for being able to not eat a cookie!

Waiting by the Door
(a poem about my daily meditation practice)

Every day I wait by the door where my beloved enters.
It is not the door to the street,
but the door to the rooftop tower.
I never ask her how she enters at that level,
as I do not want to scare her away with questions.

I wait and wait by the door, even though
I sense she slips by me several times a day,
as she is a master of subtlety and disguise.

But when I least expect it,
She suddenly appears before me in all her breathtaking
beauty.
Often I just catch a glimpse of her warm, moist, empty eyes,
before she is gone again.
Occasionally she takes a moment to sit beside me
for a bit of silent conversation.

Sometimes if I am beyond wanting anything more,
she moves like the lightest breeze
directly into my heart,
until both she and I disappear,
and the silence is left to carry on the conversation all alone.

Distinguishing Fear from Intuition

Q: I have a difficulty distinguishing between intuition and pointless fear and anxiety. I'm often flooded with emotions, and I don't know when I should follow them and when I should ignore them. For example, I often feel uneasy of something or someone. I'm unsure when I should trust my heart because it's telling me the truth and when I should ignore it because it's just my hypervigilant traumatized mind scaring me. I have made mistakes by following my feelings when I shouldn't have and ignoring them when I shouldn't have. Please give me some insight as to how to tell the difference between intuition and fear.

A: Very simply, the truth is whatever opens your heart and quiets the mind. If something has the opposite effect of contracting your heart and making your mind very busy, then it is not very true. There is always some truth to our fears and doubts, but not very much truth. In contrast, an intuition may have a lot of truth to it, and so it will have a quality of softening or opening your heart. The truth doesn't always feel good and it is not always what we might call positive, but it does always have this effect of opening the heart. For example, finding out that your romantic partner is in love with someone else will not feel good, but it will allow you to relax and be more open inside because you now know what is really going on.

In discriminating between a mind-generated fear and a deeper intuition, get curious about where the thought or feeling came from. Is the thought or feeling arising on the surface, or does it seem to be coming from somewhere much deeper? Most thoughts and feelings are triggered simply by the superficial activity of our mind. These thoughts feel ephemeral and have no depth or substantiality. When a deeper knowing is appearing, it can also trigger thoughts, but these thoughts will have a depth and solidity. This depth is being pointed to when someone says that something "rings true" or that something "hit me like a ton of bricks."

It is also helpful in determining how true an impulse is to compare it to something else. For a simple example, you might be walking at night and you have a fearful thought that "maybe I shouldn't go down that street." If you just look at that thought in isolation, it might seem to be an important message from your intuition. All there is, is truth, so even a fear that is not very true at all has a little truth. It is actually possible that something bad would happen if you walk down that street, but it might not be very likely. Again if that is all you consider, it is difficult to distinguish how true it is. But if you take a moment and imagine changing course and walking down a different street, you then have something to compare it to. You can check how your heart responds when you consider walking down the first street to how it responds when you consider walking down the second street, and even then compare it to stopping and calling a taxi. This gives you something to compare and contrast, and it will be easier to notice any shift in your heart's openness.

There are subtleties to this process in that your heart is always responding to whatever you are experiencing right now. So if you are purely imagining walking down the street, your heart will reflect how true or important or meaningful that experience is for you right now. However, if you have another thought about how you "should" be brave, or a judgment of how fearful you are, then your heart will show you how true the judgment is. With any big decision, it is helpful to give yourself as much time as possible to get a sense of the overall climate of truth of all of the possible choices, since each of the possibilities will also trigger fears and judgments that might not be very true, even if the choice itself is very true for you. And similarly, your desires and preferences may get triggered and make a choice that is not very true for you seem more compelling than it really is. Does considering that thing that you really, really want open your heart? Or is the desire actually a place of contraction? It was surprising to me when I first noticed how contracted and painful my romantic infatuations really were!

Finally, it can be helpful to be gentle with yourself. The good news is that your consciousness cannot be harmed no matter how many "wrong" choices you make. It turns out that what happens as a result of our choices is usually not that important or true. Our soul or essence is enriched by every experience in life, so the difficulties we encounter are not really so bad. You can allow yourself to explore all of this without taking it too seriously, and also be kind to yourself when you seem to make a wrong choice. The biggest truth is that your soul is fine no matter what happens in this life.

And even if we do go down some wrong streets in life, our inner guidance follows us and gently steers us back in the right direction. Your intuition is like a car's navigation system: if you don't hear it the first time, it simply calculates a new route to your destination. (You can read more about listening to your heart's inner guidance in Appendix 1.)

Boredom Is Not from Lack of Stimulation

Boredom doesn't come from a lack of stimulation or variety. Boredom is what we experience when we are not paying attention to the now. The divine mystery is always here in this and every moment. If we are giving a lot of attention to what's happening right here and right now, we will never be bored. This is good news, because it's a lot easier to give more attention to the moment just as it is than to try and drum up some excitement or drama.

Try it out. What does this moment consist of? What sounds, touches, sights, smells, and tastes are present right now? What internal experiences are you having? Are there many or few thoughts? Does your being have an emotional quality, or are your emotions quiet right now? Is there any peace, love, or joy here right now? Is there even a tiny sliver of peace? Or the slightest sense of joy? What happens if you pay very close attention to these subtle things? How is each and every element in your experience right now changing or shifting? If you pay close attention, can you actually catch the instant when a thought, feeling, sound, or sensation appears? Can you catch the exact instant when a thought, feeling, or sensation disappears?

When you are paying life this much attention, is it even possible to be bored? Or does the mystery already have everything you need to keep you entertained?

Everything Comes from the Same Source

Q: Is the manifest necessary for awareness to be aware? Am I inside me, that is, my Self as true nature? I keep feeling that Awareness and phenomena are two. What is amiss?

A: The beauty of this mystery is that one thing can appear as two or more. If you look at your fingers, there are more than one, but if you look at your whole hand, there is only one. Both are true at the same time. So there is nothing amiss when you experience two things as separate. It is just also possible to experience those same two things as one thing.

Awareness, or love, is what moves between the source of awareness and the manifest world. It can move very subtly and sense itself as awareness without an object, but most of the time awareness likes to touch, smell, taste, see, hear, or sense an object. However, it is still just one finger of the hand touching another finger of the same hand. In other words, the manifest world comes from the same source as awareness. It all comes from the same source, appears in the same space, and dissolves back into the same emptiness. So you, awareness, objects, and space itself are all inside your true Self, which is all of these and more.

The real gift of realizing the oneness is that what is in awareness is no longer that important. There is room for everything. It still matters what happens and what you do each day, but it doesn't matter very much. The source itself cannot be harmed. And when the source is recognized, then everything you need is always available. It's like the water in your faucet: once you realize it's always available, you don't need to turn the water on all the time be sure. You can experience a dry faucet and still, in essence, have all of the water you need. Whatever you're experiencing this very moment is as good as any other experience. And while you can choose a different experience, that different experience is also as good as any other experience. Your choices still matter, but they don't matter that much.

Knowing that everything is one puts the differences (and your choices) into perspective. And yet, knowing the differences keeps the oneness fresh and alive. There are infinite choices within the oneness. What an amazing journey it is to discover all the possible differences. And yet, how much easier and more relaxing the journey is when you realize the differences don't really matter. Even the difference between oneness and separation doesn't really matter. Five fingers versus one hand is just another difference within the infinite game of awareness. So you might as well enjoy the experience you are having—at least until another one shows up!

The Heart of Fear

Q: I experience paralyzing fear of being myself with almost everybody. I find more and more that the only thing is to give everything to God. The mind seems to intervene at every turn, and just makes a mess of things. I believe courage is the way forward, but every time I try to do something like acceptance, the mind claims it and turns into a diversion tactic. Does this make sense: just doing nothing, keeping my attention on being, and not letting thought steal my attention? I trust this place of stillness, and I feel I don't need anything else. I don't believe in therapy. What are your thoughts on the matter?

A: I hear you about the trickiness of the mind's resistance. If you can stay with your attention on Being, that is the simplest approach. However, there's a place for healing the mind stuff, so I wouldn't necessarily reject therapy out of hand. The key is to find a therapist and therapy with a deeply spiritual orientation.

I often say there are two aspects to the spiritual process. One is to develop contact with Essence or Being and to realize that is what you truly are. The second aspect is to heal the stuff that gets in the way of contact with Essence. The art is knowing when to just rest in Being and when to focus on and inquire into the mind stuff. Someone once said that life is one damn thing after another, but therapy is called for when it is the same damn thing over and over. So when something is reoccurring over and over, then having someone with a more objective viewpoint guide and support your inquiry is helpful.

The purpose of the inquiry is to know the truth of your experience, not necessarily to change it or fix it. The deepest healing is when we discover that there is nothing that needs to be healed. That requires a deep and subtle exploration into the heart of your fear and resistance until you know that both are not just in the way of love but are also made of love. What else but love can care enough to resist or be afraid? To bring something out of the dark, all you have to do is shine the light of awareness on it. You don't need to get rid of it or change it.

Your own heart is the truest guide in this journey. The truth is whatever opens your heart and quiets your mind. If you find that a particular therapy or practice does this, then it is true for you. If you find that the opposite is happening, then it makes sense to drop it and try something else.

What an Amazing Dance Awareness Is!

Q: Why does it seem like Awareness is one thing and the content is another thing?

A: Awareness is a fundamental quality of Being, just like wetness is a fundamental quality of water. The function of this quality of Being is to create experience. Being that is totally at rest without awareness is just what it is, with nothing happening. But when awareness arises, there is a difference or distinction and a kind of distance between one thing and another, including the distinction between the source of awareness and the content of awareness. It is because of this distance or difference that something can happen and you can experience it through awareness.

So Being steps back from itself by being aware. It's like how you cannot touch the tip of your finger with that same finger. In order to feel something with your finger, it has to be something else other than that finger itself. The awareness and the object of awareness come from the same source, so they are not really separate, just as when you look at your hand, the eye that sees your hand and your hand are not really separate. They are different, but not separate.

So Being becomes aware in order to create the space, or venue, for life to happen. It has to step back from itself as infinite Being in order to have something less than the totality of infinity to taste or see or feel. It is awareness that allows Being to step back in this way and taste, see, and feel a part of itself. Awareness allows Being to dance with itself. Without awareness there is nothing that can dance and nothing it can dance with. But with awareness, there appears to be something that dances and something that it dances with, even though they are the same Being.

Just as you might take a break from dancing to rest, Being sometimes has had enough awareness for the time being and will come to rest as pure Being, with no awareness and no content. But it is the same Being whether it is on the dance floor or taking a rest. The dancer can still dance again, and Being can still create anytime it wants to. This whole world is the dance Being is dancing right now. What an amazing dancer she is!

Choose the Best You Can Until "You" No Longer Choose

Q: If God is the doer, and the person is not the doer, then every condition of my life is fixed. So which thought should I put in my mind and which actions should I do with my body?

A: In an unevolved state of consciousness like an animal or a human acting out of their animal nature, there is little real free will or choice, since everything happens according to instinct and conditioning. Then as we evolve as humans, there is more and more free will and choice, since our self-awareness means that we can choose to act outside of instinct and conditioning. At first, most of us use our free will to try to get what we want out of life, and sometimes we succeed and sometimes we don't. In the process of exercising our free will, we develop our intellect, skills, discrimination, strength, and power.

As our discrimination improves, we notice how acting out of self-interest is actually a place of suffering, and so we begin to question our choices and even our identity on a deeper level. When we gain some sense of our own intuition and wisdom, we begin to follow it more often. As a result, our inner knowing becomes stronger, and so more and more of our choices come from there, from the innate wisdom of the Divine.

Once we realize our divine nature on a very deep level, not just intellectually, then most of our actions naturally flow from this deeper place within us. Then there is no longer any sense of having free will or choice, because now we cannot act except in accordance with our inner wisdom. Our choices become "choiceless choices." You just know what is true to do, and you do it without any possibility of acting otherwise. When I met my teacher, Neelam, I suddenly knew I was going to follow her to India even though I had no desire to go to India at the time. I wouldn't normally have chosen it, and yet deep down, I simply knew I was going.

So first there is little choice, because of our conditioning, then gradually there are more and more choices to be made, as we free ourselves from our conditioning, and eventually there are fewer and fewer choices that you make, as life and Being just make them through you.

Therefore the simplest answer for now to your question is to choose to think and do whatever seems the truest and the most aligned with your essence. This can move you further into alignment with the wisest part of you. As long as you experience that you have a choice, then you might as well use it in the most effective way to align with essence, and thereby further your spiritual evolution and growth. Use your choices to bring you to the place where you realize you no longer have any choices! To act as if there are no choices before this is fully realized is a kind of spiritual bypassing that usually doesn't work out too well. In the meantime, you can do your best to make your choices from the deepest and wisest place within you.

When we are aligned with a bigger perspective, we realize that all along everything was God's doing and God's choices. But we have to get to that realization, not just intellectually, but by grappling with life until our own discrimination, motivation, and action come from the depth of our Being. You choose the best you can until you can no longer choose any differently than your innermost heart.

Being in the Flow

Q: My experience seems to move in and out of a sense of silence, and my actions sometimes come out of the flow and sometimes out of a separate sense of "me." However, I'm seeing that I just need to do whatever is in front of me to do, just for its own sake.

A: I like your conclusion: "I just need to do whatever is in front of me to do, just for its own sake." The actions that come out of the flow don't have anything to do with the limited "me" that you sometimes experience. Rather, they are opportunities for exploring the real you. So the actions are important, but not for the reason we usually think they are.

In addition to being willing to do things just for the sake of doing them, also allow yourself to really notice and discriminate how true doing these things is and how much in the flow you feel when you are doing them—not to fix anything, but just to become very aware your experience.

It is natural that you will have genuine experiences of the silence and a sense of flow, and it is also natural that your mind will try to make that happen or question whether it is real or not. And it is natural that these two states will feel very different.

The silence and the flow are not up to you, but fully experiencing them in whatever way they are showing up is. Any shift or transformation will come out of the simplicity of just experiencing things the way they are, including all the ways they might be tight, mental, apathetic, or stuck.

Allowing things to be as they are is what heals them, although there is no formula for how quickly that occurs. What can seem like the same old reaction can actually be a deeper level of conditioning that is coming up to be seen.

By simply being with things just as they are, you also get to experience more fully the blessed moments when silence envelops you and the flow carries you gently like a newborn baby. It also becomes more and more possible to recognize that the silence and the flow are here even when the mind is busy.

Keep All of Your Anger for Yourself!

Q: I become extremely resistant when I fall into anger. I insist on my preferred story. It's like being angry and making things worse actually fulfills my story by making me more special.

A: Often with anger, we feel the need to either suppress it or express it. In both cases, we are trying to feel it less. Obviously if you suppress your anger, you are trying to feel it less. And if you express or hold onto it, the hope is that you will manage to unload it onto someone or something else and not have to feel it so much. We hold onto it to try to get to that place where we can righteously unload it. But the hope is to stop feeling it by eventually expressing it.

There is a third possibility, which is to just feel the anger without suppressing or expressing it, to just be filled with the red hot energy of anger and not do anything about it. This is usually only possible when we have become skillful at suppressing or expressing our anger so that we can regulate the level of it and not be overwhelmed by it. Once we are good at suppressing our anger, we can experiment with just letting it be there. We can discover that it is safe to be angry as long as we don't express it.

This letting it be here is a true allowing of the anger, and it also allows us to really get to know the essential nature of this energy we call anger. Most emotions are limited or distorted expressions of something more essential. In the case of anger, it is a limited or distorted experience of our essential strength. When we develop the ability to just feel very angry, the experience of anger can open up into a fuller experience of our essential strength. We can be filled with a deep sense of the limitless energy and capacity of our true nature. Feeling our true strength can bring us to a place where we no longer need to be angry, because we feel safe and capable in our own essence. This is not a suppression of anger, but a discovery of something bigger and more complete.

Practically speaking, because anger and strength are big, energetic experiences, giving them lots of space helps. Specifically with anger, it can help to let the anger be bigger than your body. Because we identify with our body, when "I" feel angry, there is a tendency to hold the anger inside the body. But you can simply let it fill the space all around you. If necessary, you can let the anger be bigger than the entire neighborhood, or bigger than the entire country you are in. This can make it much easier to let the anger be there in all of its red hot glory. Imagine what would happen if you tried to hold an entire volcano inside you! Then imagine how much easier it would be to contain a volcano if you just let it rest within the entire solar system. Then there is no problem with the nature of a volcano, since there is plenty of space for it to be a volcano.

Everything we experience is always an opportunity to discover more about our true nature, including every emotion and feeling. You might as well get to know your anger instead of trying to get rid of it or be free of it. You may discover it is a wonderful resource you can enjoy, embrace, and integrate into your true identity as limitless Being. Then it would be silly to dissipate it, when you can keep it all for yourself!

Sex Is Great, and Yet It's Not All It's Cracked Up to Be

Q: Yesterday I had a beautiful meditation, and then I began to notice sexual energy arising. The energy seemed to occupy nonsexual parts of my body, such as my hands, arms, and legs. Various muscles in these parts were also twitching a bit, especially in my hands. I am wondering what this experience might be indicating and what might be a path to follow toward properly dealing with it or accepting it.

I did a few web searches and came across a lot of discussion of kundalini and tantric teachings that seemed somewhat relevant. In my web searches, some of the language described sexual desire as one of the major obstacles toward awakening. Should I be ridding myself of or letting go of all sexual desire? Is that something that is actually possible given human nature? Was the fact that the sensations were in nonsexual parts of my body an indication of some type of harnessing of sexual energy that can somehow be useful toward awakening?

A: First of all, the energy experiences you are describing are very normal and typical. Unusual and sometimes strong energies appearing in the body is a natural and common experience as our awareness opens up. There is no need to determine if it is sexual energy or some other energy, as there is not really a difference. We are used to describing energy in our sexual organs as sexual energy simply because sexual activity often follows when energy is localized there.

But the same energy in your hands or limbs may or may not be associated with sexuality, mostly depending on your expectations and how you describe the experience. If you tell a sexual story about the energy, then it will probably feel that way, and may then move more into your sexual centers. If you describe it as kundalini or some kind of spiritual energy, then it will seem to be more spiritual in nature. The meaning of the energy is the meaning you give it.

While you can explore this energy from a tantric perspective, there is a simpler approach that works very well. You can just let the energy do whatever it does and let go of managing it in any way. There is a divine intelligence in this energy that knows what it is doing, so you can just let it unfold and do whatever it is doing. You don't need to figure it out, increase it, decrease it, hold onto it, get rid of it, or worry if it gets stronger or goes away. The energy will unfold in the most healthy and beneficial way if you just allow it to be. The most helpful perspective is to simply trust that everything is unfolding just as it needs to, and so then you can be curious about and open to whatever happens next. In this context, letting the energy be bigger than your body can relieve the pressure to act, so that you can more fully allow it to unfold organically. Your only job then is to be very attentive to what happens each moment. If there is some way in which this energy relates to or can serve your awakening, it will be revealed by simply being curious about it.

As to the place sexuality holds in one's spiritual unfoldment, I would suggest that sex is a natural and normal part of the human experience but not that important in relation to realizing our deeper nature as Essence or Being. In some ways, having a body is like having a wild animal as a pet. Ideally, if you have a wild animal as a pet, you would do everything you could to allow the wild animal at times to be wild, while at the same time you would create appropriate limits on when and where it could express its wild nature. So you might give that animal a large enclosure to roam around in, but you wouldn't let it roam around your neighborhood when it might end up eating your neighbors' pets!

Similarly, a balanced perspective on your sexuality recognizes that sex is a natural and healthy expression of the animal part of your Being, and so that would include finding appropriate ways to express it. The results have not been good when spiritual groups try to repress or deny sexuality, for example, the Catholic priesthood. Nevertheless, sexuality is a very strong force, and so there is some wisdom to putting limits on its expression, just like you might want a strong fence around your pet mountain lion! These limits are both practical (they can keep you out of prison!) and they help direct your exploration of your life experience to include the deeper realities of your Essence or true nature.

Sexuality, in and of itself, is not an obstacle to awakening, but a strong attachment or addiction to sex can be. Any strong attachment or addiction can be an obstacle to awakening, so sex is not any different in this regard. It is the strong attachment or addiction that is the obstacle, not sexuality itself. Nevertheless, strong attachments and addictions are tremendous opportunities to see the deeper truth that our resistance and grasping are what cause us to suffer, not our experience. Even attachment isn't a mistake, since it is through our attachments that we discover the nature of attachment.

All there is, is Essence. Anything and everything is included in your true nature because you *are* everything. So there is no need to deny or avoid any experience. But you have also been given the capacity to discriminate how important and true different experiences are. So a wise and healthy approach to sexuality includes discriminating how important and meaningful sex really is, and then giving it the appropriate space and attention. It is not an exact formula, and there is no harm if you overdo it or underdo it in a particular moment. In fact, if there is the opportunity, in a healthy and mutual way, to overdo it sexually, go for it! The balance comes in the overall place sex has in your life and on your spiritual path.

The bigger question is always, "Are you in touch with Essence in this moment, whether you are being sexual or not?" Sexual experience that is not connected to love and tenderness is not that satisfying, while an experience of tender loving connectedness is deeply satisfying even when it is not at all sexual. Sex is beautiful and amazing, and yet it is not all that it is cracked up to be. Enjoy it when you can and also pursue the bigger questions of life and your true nature.

Meet Life with Everything You've Got

Q: Your book talks about being in a state of not knowing. If I focus on not knowing, how do I deal with situations in my daily life. I'm a veterinarian. My rational mind formulates data (symptoms, etc), makes plans for treatment, and predicts outcome (prognosis). How can I be in this mindset and at the same time be in a not-knowing state of mind?

A: It is not a question of being in both mindsets simultaneously, but a matter of being flexible and able to switch from one mindset to the other as needed. When you need your rational mind and the knowledge and skills you have as a veterinarian, then being able to focus and formulate data and plans is what is called for. However, your rational mind is limited and might even get in the way in other moments.

Even in your professional role, there might be moments when your mind alone cannot serve your patients and their owners. When a beloved pet is at the end of its life, and any further medical treatment would just prolong suffering, then it can best serve your patients to just be present in a place of not-knowing with the mystery of death and loss. In a moment like that, our heartfelt compassion and pure awareness is what is needed.

In the context of your spiritual unfoldment, the mind is a powerful but limited tool. Trying to figure out the biggest mysteries with the mind is like using the same tool for every task. A hammer is great for driving in nails, but what good is it for opening a jar of pickles? Or brushing your teeth? Or enjoying a sunset? In some situations, you need to put down the hammer and either pick up another tool or just be with your experience without any tools or techniques. Similarly, there are times it is appropriate to focus the mind, and other times it is more useful to drop into the heart, or even beyond the heart into the emptiness of pure spacious awareness.

Use your mind whenever it is useful, and then let go of it when it is not useful. It isn't necessary to stop the mind, but more a question of holding your thoughts and beliefs lightly and being curious about what else is here besides your thoughts. A closed mind is only useful when it already has the information or answers needed in that moment. An open mind can look beyond its own limited knowledge to meet the uniqueness of a new moment and even touch the infinite.

Transcendence includes everything. Your rational mind is a beautiful mystery and a powerful tool, but there is much more to life that the rational mind is not able to penetrate. In exploring the deeper mysteries, our minds can pose the inquiry questions and even direct awareness inward, but then we need to allow the place of not-knowing to take over. It is only when we stay open and curious with the intensity and immensity of Being that a deeper kind of knowing can arise. Like when you can't remember a name, and when you stop trying, it pops into your mind, a deeper insight often appears only after you've given up thinking about it.

This life is full of challenges and deep abiding mysteries. Why not meet it with everything you have got? You have a good mind, a beautiful heart, and a limitless Being. Why not use them all in your daily life and in your spiritual journey?

What a Long Strange Trip It's Been

I just had an interesting email conversation with a new friend about the importance of flexibility in our consciousness and how the idea of "better" can be limiting if it is believed too rigidly. Here is my most recent message to him:

Advaita and also the idea that there is no better or worse, are pointing to very big truths. It can be very expansive and liberating to see how there is ultimately only one thing here and how there is really no better or worse. This is especially liberating if we have been stuck for a while in a more limited view of separation and in a desperate search for a "better" life.

But then you can get stuck in "It is all one" and "There is no better or worse." True flexibility means being able to see the bigger truths and to also be able to contract down to a limited identity as a separate somebody, and so to also be able to practically and functionally work to make things "better." The ideal is to move freely between these polarities. Then you can work to make things better and also accept when it doesn't work. Or you can sometimes just rest deeply for a while in the place where it is all perfect.

Most people are more stuck in the limited, smaller viewpoints, which is probably why a lot of spiritual teachers and teachings point to a bigger viewpoint. But the biggest freedom is when you can move freely between any and all viewpoints. Then it doesn't really matter what viewpoint you are experiencing, because you know deep down that it is just a viewpoint, and it will change again soon anyway.

I also sense that the smaller ideas, viewpoints, and identities are all contained in the biggest truths. Transcendence includes everything, and doesn't leave anything out. Awareness can be like a zoom lens and either focus in on a part of the whole or zoom out and take in more of the complete whole. But in either case, the smaller part of the bigger reality still exists. Even our thoughts have a kind of existence as neurons firing in our brain, although that existence is a much smaller and briefer one than we usually realize (and so thoughts are much less important than we usually think).

Most of our "problems" result from thinking that a small truth is bigger and more important than it really is. When we are zoomed in, our problems (and our thoughts, ideas, worries, beliefs, fears, hopes, and wishes) look much bigger than they really are, just like when we are looking in a microscope. A zoomed in perspective has its place, but when we get stuck there, we lose perspective. Although it is rare, I also encounter people who are stuck in the zoomed out perspective, which can be liberating at first but limiting when zooming in and focusing is needed.

For example, for years I had a hobby as an audiophile. It was fun to tweak my system to try and get a better sound, although mostly I found that if I changed something it just sounded different, not really better. What I thought was better was always changing. The real trick was to enjoy the journey and not get attached to the results, and for that it is helpful to take a step back and zoom out. In those moments, I often felt a deep appreciation for every experience and everything I had tried with my headphones. It reminded me of the beauty and mystery of hearing and music and electronics and everything else. Being zoomed out then also freed me to zoom in and become curious again about how tweaking the system some other way might alter the sound.

So it is possible to have the experience of something being better or worse, and it is also possible to have the experience that this is all one reality, which embraces all of the mysterious effects that occur whenever we change even the slightest thing in our environment. As an album title says, "What a long strange trip it's been" —and most likely will continue to be!

Proof of Oneness

Q: I'm trying to find some evidence that nonduality is a better model than duality. I can't find any. The idea that reality is one unified field and can be experienced as such is interesting, but so are pink elephants. The word evidence implies objectivity. When I see so-called great sages of the nonduality community demonstrating objective evidence of addiction and disease, I'm finding that the standard of evidence seems to be nothing more than belief. I've even heard that the ultimate standard of evidence is the happiness of the seeker. Since happiness comes and goes in duality also, that doesn't seem to be a reliable standard either. I do understand that if duality is a bogus position, then examining the nature of reality from such a position has special problems, but evidence that nonduality is our true nature should not be nonexistent if it is the truth.

A: My own sense is that duality and nonduality are not really opposites. Instead they are part of a spectrum of truth or reality. Nonduality is the larger truth that contains all of duality and more. This can possibly explain some or many of the paradoxes, including the sad but real truth that many teachers who have to some degree realized the bigger truth of oneness can still express in a less than healthy or enlightened way at the level of duality. Their experience of the bigger truth is real, and their unhealthy actions in the world are real also. No need to deny either one nor to assume that one negates the other (or excuses the other).

I will share that my own realizations of oneness have made me happier than anything else I have ever experienced. And they are powerful enough in and of themselves to be all of the evidence I will personally ever need. This is not scientific proof, but it is suggestive and evocative that so many people have reported a similar experience. It is a different kind of evidence, even if it doesn't fit our usual scientific model of evidence. I guess it is more of a subjective form of evidence instead of objective, but perhaps even subjective and objective are not really opposites but rather a spectrum of different amounts of truth. In this case, a lot of subjective evidence can add up to as much as a little objective evidence.

Q: If nonduality is the true nature of consciousness, then it must have somehow been forgotten. Maybe it's this way so that duality can appear. Otherwise we would have no objects or objectiveness. That maybe explains the condition of the illusory "I." The seeming existence of a universe external to ourselves depends on it. So how does the "I" disappear? And can the "I" disappear and knowingness or beingness still be present? I know you have spent a good many years studying all this, and you seem to be convinced. Maybe the sense of "I" just shifts to something that cannot be known by the illusory, limited, separate "I" ahead of time? So how does it happen? I have looking for objective evidence to destroy the belief in the limited "I." Is this the wrong approach?

A: Again, duality and nonduality are not really opposites. Duality is just the experience of a smaller part of nonduality. The bigger truth is always here whether we are experiencing it or not, just as the entire room you are in is still here even if you limit your experience of it by putting your hands around your eyes like a pair of blinders.

The "I" is also not the opposite of the universal knowingness. It is simply a small part of it. Since the "I" is just a thought, it is a very temporary form within this larger ocean of consciousness. Thought is the mechanism by which we focus or contract our awareness to experience the separate self and the world it appears in. But it is still just a thought

There is no method or technique that can cause the sense of identity to shift from the small idea of self to the larger reality it arises in. It is something that happens to us, not something we do.

It is wonderful that you are looking so passionately for the truth. I suggest that you start looking more at subjective truth also. What is your actual experience of the "I" right now? Where is it located? Does it move around? Where are you noticing its location from? Does the sense of "I" stay within your body all of the time? Is it sometimes bigger than and sometimes smaller than your body? Where do your senses actually exist? Are they inside of you, outside of you, or both? Where do thoughts come from? What is the source of your awareness? Questions like these cannot be answered objectively, but they can be answered subjectively.

Q: So there is no objective reality. Reality is, by its nature, subjective and probabilistic. The term "objective" merely identifies those things that are highly probable independent of time and space.

A: Yes, there is no completely objective evidence or reality, but it is a useful concept or term to describe something that has more truth, reality, evidence or, as you say, probability than something that has less truth, which we might then call subjective. All subjective evidence has some truth or reality to it, even if it is only real as a thought in someone's mind.

A lot of things we conceive of as opposites are really just different degrees of one thing, such as light and dark. The one thing that exists is light or photons, but dark is a useful concept for describing the situation where there is little or almost no light. Similarly, objective and subjective are just part of the spectrum of truth. Truth is what exists, and some observations or experiences contain more truth and some contain less, but they all contain some, no matter how subjective. In a sense, an objective truth is just an observation or experience that contains a lot of subjective truth, such as when several people subjectively observe the same thing. Therefore, you could say that all objective truth is made up of subjective truth.

You might find the bigger truth you are seeking if you start including every smaller subjective truth you can discover. A lot of small truths put together can add up to a big truth!

Your Minimum Daily Requirement of Contradictions

Spiritual teachings can be wonderfully contradictory, and this can be good for us in creating greater flexibility of awareness. We should all have a minimum daily dose of contradictory ideas. Here are a few conversations that explore the opportunities in contradictions further:

Q: Having read widely on spiritual matters, I have come to a conflicting impasse. We are told by the metaphysicians of the world that through the Law of Attraction our thoughts have a powerful energy (vibration) and that we attract what we notice and expect. We are told time and time again to expect positive things and then that is what you will attract.

That said, spiritual masters will often state that at a soul level there is no such thing as good or bad as defined by our limited minds. The latter suggest there is only experience, and all experience is welcomed.

Empirical evidence seems to agree with the spiritual masters, as notwithstanding our grand intentions in positive thought we seem to suffer outcomes that are often contrary to our thoughts. One just needs to review the massive fall out of many positive individuals who had their entire financial wealth wiped out by the 2008 financial crisis. It would appear in that case that no amount of positive thinking would have changed the situation for these individuals and, in fact, they may have been too positive in their thoughts, never expecting such a loss!

Furthermore, at a soul level we can possibly make choices for human incarnation that quite often will involve suffering and hardship necessary for soul experience and development. It appears to me that there exists a conflict between soul level and mind level. What is it that I am missing? Is there a reconciliation between the two schools of spiritual teaching?

A: The two perspectives are complementary rather than contradictory. They are both pointing to a part of the truth. However, I will add that just because both perspectives have some truth, that doesn't mean they are equally true. The perspective that our soul or essence is enriched by every experience, and so may even choose difficult experiences is the bigger truth. It is such a big truth that the smaller truth that the metaphysicians share about how our thoughts affect reality operates within the bigger truth of the perfection of all experiences. In a sense they are different levels of truth, and yet the bigger truth is so big that it contains the smaller truth.

To me, the ideal is not to hold one perspective or another but to, instead, have the flexibility to move in and out of all perspectives. For example, since you are experiencing a human life, you might as well do everything possible on a practical level to make your life better. If you find it helpful to set goals, take action, and even focus the energy of your thoughts, then why not try it and see what happens? Then in the event that your soul has a different idea of what would be better for you in this lifetime, it all becomes an opportunity to surrender and feel gratitude for things just as they are.

The art is in knowing when to hold each perspective, but that can only be learned by trying both and seeing what happens. Someone once suggested that success is the natural result of massive amounts of failure. So no matter what happens when you hold a particular perspective, you can use the resulting experience to learn to be more curious and discriminating about what perspective might be the most functional in each new moment.

Q: Is it okay to let someone harm others? It seems that if we were enlightened, we would perceive everything as one, so we would just let someone harm others without attachment.

A: This is a common question because it's confusing to the mind when two opposite things are both true. So while it is true that everything is one and there's nothing that can harm consciousness, it's also true that you can act without attachment in a situation such as the one you described.

Here's a simple metaphor to illustrate how two opposite things can be true: On a rainy day, you experience thick clouds and some rain. And yet, above the clouds, the bigger truth is that the sun is still shining. I call it a "bigger truth" because the sun shines on the entire earth, not just on the clouds above your head, and the sun shining is more constant and long lasting than a rainstorm. However, just because it's true that the sun is still shining (behind the clouds) during a rainstorm doesn't mean you go out in your bathing suit and some sunscreen to work on your tan! Your experience of clouds and rain is still real, so you may want to wear a raincoat instead.

When it comes to the hurt and violence in this world, the bigger truth is that consciousness is not harmed by the pain and suffering. Yet while this is true, the pain is still real, and it may be possible to do something to prevent or stop the violent or hurtful act or at least to help soothe or heal a person who's already suffered from such harm.

Knowing the bigger truth, that there is no lasting harm, can free us to respond to whatever is happening. There's nothing to lose, so why not help someone if you can? The value of this bigger perspective is that it can allow us to see the hurt and violence but not be traumatized or overwhelmed by it. When we don't see the bigger truth, our reaction to the pain in the world is often to avoid or deny it because the pain can seem too horrible to acknowledge. Seeing the bigger truth allows us to better respond to pain and is also likely to make us more willing to respond.

Realizing that love and peace are still present even in such situations—that they are always here "behind the clouds"—unlocks our capacity to be compassionate toward the victims of violence and even toward the perpetrators. This may allow us to stop someone from being violent in a loving and compassionate way. In contrast, responding to violence with more violence usually just breeds more violence.

When it rains, it's not the end of the world. The sun is still shining and will eventually come out from behind the clouds. You don't need to overreact to the rain, while you still might take appropriate actions to stay dry. And even if you do get wet, it's often not that big a deal.

Q: In one of your talks, you mentioned that our true nature as the space of awareness cannot be affected by anything, and you used the example that even an atom bomb going off in a room would not in any way affect the space in the room. Yet a couple of minutes earlier in the same presentation, you said that awareness becomes powerfully imprinted by things which it becomes aware of, and you used the example of a baby duck becoming imprinted with the first thing it sees at the time of its birth, whether it is the mother duck or a laboratory scientist. Are these two statements reconciled in the same way that Nisargadatta Maharaj spoke about a distinction between consciousness (which perhaps in your presentation might be that which becomes imprinted) and awareness (that which he termed "prior to consciousness")?

A: I love it when someone points out contradictions in my own words! Life and Being are rich and mysterious, and so to capture all of it in words requires that you contradict yourself a lot.

I often speak about different levels of truth. In this case, the biggest truth is that the source of awareness (what Nisargadatta is calling awareness in your reference above) is not ever affected or harmed by anything. But awareness (what Nisargadatta is calling consciousness) is an outward expression of that source, and it is affected by everything it encounters. That is why we call it awareness, which is simply the ability to have an experience, perception, or knowledge of something that is happening. In order to have perception, experience, or knowledge, we have to be affected by what is happening. If it has no effect on us, there can be no awareness.

The important thing is to realize that the source of awareness cannot be harmed and so any effect that things have on our awareness is always temporary and not ultimately that important. When this is realized, it can free us to enjoy everything that affects our awareness (meaning everything that happens to us) and not worry about the temporary impact any of it has. This is a very big freedom indeed.

Even the imprinting I speak of is temporary. All imprinting, karma, *vasanas, samskaras,* and conditioning get dissolved eventually, so they are all temporary. You can hold all of it lightly even as you inquire sincerely to understand it all more deeply.

I wrote more about this in an article, which is included below.

You Cannot Be Harmed

Consciousness is affected by experience but not harmed. It is the nature of aware consciousness to be affected by everything it experiences. Every color and sound, every event and experience, and every passing thought or feeling affects your consciousness. That is why we call it consciousness. A rock isn't as affected by these things, so we consider a rock less conscious than a person.

And yet, consciousness is not harmed by anything. That is its nature, that it can't be harmed. The form of anything can be harmed or permanently changed. Your body can be harmed, but the consciousness that contains your body cannot be harmed.

This is good news. It's like a "Get out of Jail" card in Monopoly. No matter what happens, you, as consciousness, are completely unharmed. What a relief! There is nothing that can harm you. No one and nothing has ever harmed you.

This is not to say that consciousness isn't affected deeply by both the good and bad things that happen to us. Every hurtful and unkind act leaves an impression in the consciousness of those involved. It's just that the impression doesn't permanently limit or damage the awareness of those involved. If something permanently affects us, it could be said to have harmed us. But if the effect is temporary, then what is the ultimate harm? Everything that profoundly affects our awareness, from the beautiful to the tragic, eventually passes. It is the miracle of our consciousness that it can heal from any wound, even if our body cannot.

What you are is eternal, aware space, or consciousness. You have a body, but you are not that body. So while your body can be permanently harmed, just like your car or camera can be, you as consciousness eventually heal or recover from every experience that has affected you. Even if the effect lasts for lifetimes, eventually it is diminished and disappears. From the perspective of something eternal, even many lifetimes isn't that long.

When you realize that your true nature as consciousness can't be harmed, that puts all of life's difficulties in perspective. Similarly, when someone's car is totaled in an accident but he or she isn't hurt, we consider that person lucky. This is because we have a perspective on the relative importance of damage to a car. It's not such a big deal relative to a serious physical injury or death. If you realize that you are aware space, then everything else is like the totaled car — no big deal.

Some things are still more important than others. Physical harm is still a bigger difficulty than harm to a car or other physical object. But by knowing that your true nature is space, which cannot be harmed, the bigger difficulties and even tragedies in life can be seen in perspective.

A simple question to ask is, "What effect does this experience have on my eternal soul?" While everything leaves an impression on your awareness and your soul, nothing can ever permanently harm your soul, your true nature as empty awareness. In fact, every experience enriches your soul. Every moment adds to the depth and richness of your deepest knowing. We sense this in people who have faced a lot of difficulty in life and who have accepted their fate. There is a depth and wisdom that only comes from a wide range of experience, including painful and unwelcome experiences.

The willingness to meet and have any experience comes from the recognition that what you are is open, spacious awareness. Your body, mind, personality, emotions, and desires all appear within that awareness, but they are not you. And the real you cannot be harmed.

Suffering Is Not a Mistake

Q: Could we say that there are two aspects of the same one awareness--one aspect that suffers from experiences and one that never suffers? It seems that suffering might be eternal with or without realization of one's true nature, although you say that the suffering gets dissolved eventually. So do you have any particular insights to share about the 'eventually' part, since our true nature is said to be beyond/without any relationship to time altogether?

A: My own sense of the "eventually" part of the story is that since our true nature is not harmed by suffering, the eternal aspect of our being just keeps on trucking in and out of all kinds of identifications, attachments, imprinting, and sufferings before and after any kind of spiritual realization. Eternity is a lot of time to fill up, and so it gets very creative at generating new and unexplored dimensions of experience to try on for size.

Suffering is just a particular movement of our consciousness and is not really a problem or a mistake. It is just a part of the game to make it seem like a problem. Suffering is just the movement of desire or avoidance, but this can become very subtle. Is it suffering if you are enjoying desire itself? I find the closer I get to fully experiencing my own suffering, the less suffering there is. I'm not sure exactly where the line is between suffering and not suffering, but lots of activity that continues after a spiritual realization may look like suffering on the outside but not really be experienced that way on the inside.

This is a very dynamic and fluctuating experience. To me, the ideal is not to reach some place of expansion and disidentification that is free of all suffering and creating. Instead the ideal is a flexibility to identify and disidentify, to desire and to release desires, to suffer and to also discover the joy in suffering itself, without getting stuck anywhere. Just looking around, it seems that Being as a whole is not in any rush to be completely done with anything. Given the incredible variety of experience, it seems to be enjoying its flexibility to the max!

Since eternity has no beginning and no end, maybe we can see this moment, just as it is, as the fullest expression of existence possible. Maybe "eventually" doesn't really matter because in eternity we are always already there! This experience and this moment are just as valuable to our deepest Being as every other moment and every other experience to come. Yes, spiritual realization and shifts in our degree of suffering are different experiences, but maybe they are not really any better—just different. To a completely invulnerable Being living in an eternal universe, the only thing that matters is differences. Since nothing matters really, awareness makes it "matter" by uncovering differences. The most dramatic differences are created by identification and disidentification, and the desires at the root of our suffering. If you change who you experience yourself as, you change everything. If you change what you want, you change almost everything. So Being plays with desiring and creating and striving and seeking and all of the infinite ways it can suffer and then not suffer. Again, with so much time on its hands, why wouldn't Being try it every which way?

If the ultimate is the flexibility to have any identity and any possible experience, then everyone is already experiencing some aspect of this ultimate reality. Even getting stuck in some identity or place of suffering is one of the aspects our true nature is free to explore. And since we are speaking about eternity, no one is ever stuck forever.

Ultimate freedom is not somewhere we get to, it is a place we have always been exploring and are never done exploring. Ultimate freedom is dancing as the experience you are having right now.

How Big or Small You Feel Is Not About You!

Q: How do we discern the difference between egoic self-sabotage and the heart's "no"? For example, when something doesn't feel right, though in its externals it looks to be of advantage, how do you know when the feeling is egoic fear, a tendency toward self-sabotage, or the heart saying "not for you, not now," or even "not bad, though not without some trouble."

We make many decisions each day, and many of these are a combination of Truth and illusion. This leads the sensitive to a position of vigilance and low-level anxiety. As Jung said, "Could there be a more uncomfortable position intellectually than that of floating in the thin air of unproved possibilities, not knowing whether what one sees is truth or illusion?"

A: The biggest perspective is that there is only truth and only Presence, so whatever you are seeing is pure divine presence, and that is what you really are. So even when the illusion gets pretty scary and confusing, it is still divine Presence. My favorite definition of illusion is that an illusion is something real that appears to be something other than what it really is. All illusion is the one Being appearing as all of this stuff.

Remembering this biggest truth can allow you to relax and hold everything lightly. Even if you misread every intuition and deeper sense of the right direction in life, you are never really lost. At any moment, no matter how difficult or painful the moment is, you can stop and sense the pure Presence that is at the heart of it all.

It is from this place of holding things lightly that we are also able to sometimes catch the subtle clues coming from our inner guidance. If you listen to your heart hoping that it will somehow make your life easy and make everything turn out the way you want it to, that is not a place of holding everything lightly. If you listen to your heart just to listen to your heart, you will find that it is a rewarding activity in and of itself. This is when you also happen to sense the nudge to step back just before a big wave that would otherwise have knocked you over.

As for your specific question, the difference between an egoic fear and a clear heart knowing that something is just not the best choice right now is that when it is an egoic fear, you feel small, vulnerable, and inadequate. When it is a deeper knowing, you feel normal size or even expanded and have a sense that whatever does happen, you will be able to adequately respond. If it is a very deep insight and intuition, then you might even feel very expanded and a profound sense of your own ultimate invulnerability. This is not a rigid, hard invulnerability, but a flexible, comfortable sense that you are big enough and capable enough to handle the situation easily.

I invite you to read Appendix 1, as it can take a while for this subtle and yet radical shift in perspective to really sink in: How big and adequate you feel is not telling you how big and adequate you are, instead it is telling you how big and adequate your perspective or knowing is in that particular moment. When this is truly grasped, it turns the world inside out and upside down. How big you feel is not about you! What a strange concept, and yet how freeing when you discover that how big you feel, how expanded or contracted your own sense of yourself is in this moment, is just a way your awareness distinguishes and discriminates the world around you. It is almost as if you were having someone else's sensations and feelings. If you didn't realize they were someone else's sensations, then that would be very confusing. Similarly, if you think your sense of yourself is about you, then that is equally confusing. When you realize that how big and adequate you feel is not about you, but about the relative balance between the truth and any beliefs and conditioning that just happen to be triggered in that moment, then the confusion is resolved.

The key element is how literally big, adequate, and even okay and worthy you sense your own self to be in this moment. Fear reduces that sense, makes you feel small like a young child, and contracts your awareness, including your awareness that everything is going to be fine no matter what. A deep knowing, even a deep knowing that you need to leave a situation or relationship in order to be safe doesn't take away the sense that you are capable and that everything will be alright. It can expand your awareness and give you the sense that you are bigger than your body. And it can increase the knowing that everything will be alright even as life appears to be falling apart.

As I mentioned, even if you miss these signals and make the apparently wrong choice, the stakes are not that high. Your eternal soul will still be fine. All of the hurt and difficulty will eventually be used by your true nature as food for your soul. From the soul's perspective, these daily decisions are not that important even if you totally blow it and get killed. For the soul, that is no great loss. It just carries on in its journey as if it just dropped a penny down a sewer drain.

The real gift of listening to your heart and sensing these expansions and contractions of your awareness is not in making your life easier or avoiding the numerous pitfalls in life including the biggest pitfalls, although it can sometimes help a bit with that. The real gift is that if you develop this habit of listening to your heart, then you may be listening someday when a powerful sense of your infinite eternal nature and completely transparent invulnerability arises, and you suddenly know that this deepest knowing is true beyond any doubt. These bigger knowings are the ones that transform us and fulfill our deepest longing for the truth. Following your heart in the moment to moment affairs of life simply makes you more available and trusting when a really big knowing appears.

In the meantime, you can notice and trust whatever sense of self you have in this moment. As you point out, many moments are a mix of truth and illusion. In those moments, the sense of self will be somewhere in between the contracted sense of self, you naturally experience when you are completely lost in the mind's fearful projections, and the profoundly expanded sense of self, which comes when you are having an epiphany or an awakening. A medium-sized sense of self is just a reflection of a medium-sized perspective. The good news is that you are always having the correct sense of yourself. You are always being shown how big the truth of your perspective is right now.

I would add that if you trust the moments where you know that everything is alright and will always be alright, then the other moments when you are "floating in the thin air of unproved possibilities, not knowing whether what one sees is truth or illusion" are actually a wonderful adventure. Knowing is not something we have to have ahead of time.

Instead, knowing is something we can unfold gradually like an elaborate meal or a long stroll through a botanical garden. As long as we remember that illusion can't harm us, then we can enjoy the dance between truth and illusion, knowing and not knowing to the max!

The Only Weatherman You Need

Q: If someone has low self-esteem, confidence, and self-love and has not awakened to true nature, what can be done? Even if we have had tastes of Presence, it is not much use if we are suffering deeply and are caught badly in the snare of mind, where we are barely functional and there is no sign of any significant spiritual shift in the cards. Must we have a healthy and functional ego/mind before we can hope to be free of that false identity?

I have heard some teachers insinuate or flat-out declare that so-called mental illness need not be an obstacle to awakening — and others that it is. I've also heard similar comments regarding anti-depressant and anxiety meds for example. And that we seekers should not expect spiritual pursuits to address mental, emotional, and life issues, even if spirituality may end up helping in these areas to one degree or another.

I have heard some teachers say that the spiritual path can be used as an escape from the things that hound us in our lives, that we can cherry-pick aspects of teachings and also interpret teachings in such a way that suits our neuroses, for example, remaining single or celibate or only associating with like-minded/interested people or clinging to a teacher as a parental replacement.

A: There are people whose spiritual life benefits from psychotherapy and medication, while others are able to awaken without such help, even while suffering from very painful and difficult conditioning. Similarly, some people are freed by spiritual teachings and practices, while others are caught by the same words and methods in a net of the ego.

There is no formula that works for everyone. And yet, every formula works for someone. This is why you can hear seemingly contradictory statements from different teachers and even from the same teacher! They may be speaking generally from their own experience or they may be speaking specifically to what they see happening in a particular student or seeker.

All there is, is truth. Every perspective has at least a small part of truth to it. But there is no perspective that can be put into words that contains all of the truth, or even all of the truth about even one question, such as what to do about neurosis.

This is why I point to using your own heart to discriminate the truth. The truth is whatever opens your heart (or your sense of yourself) and quiets your mind in the moment. Something that is less true tends to contract your heart and sense of being while making your mind busier. This is a completely dynamic, ever-changing equation that is different for every person in each new moment of their lives. It is also always relative: for one person a process that heals and clears emotions may provide a wonderful expansion of their perspective and capacity to feel Presence, while for another the same process may result in the opposite.

Therefore, the important question is: What is true for *you* right here and right now at this particular point in your own spiritual unfoldment? Do the practices, therapeutic approaches, and teachings you are involved with now generally open your heart, expand your sense of being, and quiet your mind? Or do they generally have the opposite effect? It helps to notice the general overall effect, as every practice or therapy will have moments that are more or less expansive, in part because any practice or therapy will also trigger conditioned reactions to the process. The best question is: What is the overall effect of your involvement with a particular teaching or therapeutic approach? Does psychotherapy with a particular therapist open you up even more to big truths, or does it wrap you up even tighter in your pain? Does a particular antidepressant free you from a neurochemical imbalance and allow you to do spiritual inquiry and exploration, or does the medicine cause a contraction of your awareness, making you less aware of everything, including your pain and your deeper nature?

It is also possible that the biggest truth is a combination of different truths. There is a tendency when a big truth is seen to use it to discount or ignore the smaller truths. This can lead to a situation where the smaller truth suddenly becomes unavoidable because it has been neglected. I often ask people who say that since there is no separate self, there is no need whatsoever for healing, where they would draw the line? If there is no need to actively address an emotional wound, does that mean there is no need to address a physical wound also? You can see the limitation of using a big truth to negate a smaller truth if you take an exaggerated example: would it make sense to just let someone bleed to death because, after all, "There is no one who dies"?

Conversely, it is also obviously limiting to ignore or negate a bigger truth. I have found it a more effective and balanced approach to work with psychological issues within a bigger spiritual perspective. It is often when we are shifting in and out of the different levels of truth that the most profound transformations happen. If we have both feet in the reliving of our traumatic experiences, then reliving or exploring the pain often just re-traumatizes us. And if we have both feet in an experience of the Absolute, the experience may be profound, but it doesn't usually release or heal our conditioning. It is when we have one foot in both dimensions, or when we are shifting in and out of both perspectives, that the potential for lasting healing and transcendence is the greatest.

Agony and Beyond and Back to Agony Again

Q: I am consumed and entirely identified with just wanting the agony of this illness to end. It is nearly unrelenting. So I want it to stop. Sometimes I want to be healthier in order that it might stop. Other times I think I've had enough and want to be dead.

I find it very hard to be in the present with this magnitude of agony or present to the desire or present at all. It hurts my head to even direct my attention one way or another. So then the mind concludes, as it has also sometimes been told by practitioners, that neurology runs the show, and there is no freedom to be found truth-wise until there is some relief — because there's just no room in the agony-filled horizon for anything else. But I don't want to believe that. But the simple practices of investigation do hurt my head more.

I liked where you said whatever we think or do, Mystery is directing it all anyway, and we aren't really making choices and that our thoughts and feelings aren't even ours but come through the way antennas pick up radio signals, so we are not to be blamed even for our fear, which in my case is rampant.

But then there are pointers about making better choices from the heart rather from thoughts, emotions, or desires. And I want to make those better choices! But wow, stillness and I seem to have parted company so long ago. So that part seemed contradictory. Don't know if I spelled out the contradiction very well--that on the one hand Mystery is doing the choosing whatever we attribute our choices too--thought, emotion, desire. And on the other hand, we'll make better choices if it comes from the heart or Silence or Mystery.

And I want to mention how much I get the message from everyone around me that thoughts cause suffering, not only to the thinking mind, but directly to the body. I'm continually being told to think more uplifting thoughts, or I can't get better unless I believe I can, or it's my self-image that's the problem.

And I looked at one of the websites you sent, which said that all illness was caused by trauma and conditioning, except where injury and poisoning are concerned. The latter two--poisoning and injury--are definitely major players for me. But I certainly can imagine that trauma and conditioning are as well. Only those are illusory, right? That's the past. So--and I don't mean to be challenging here... just desperate!--why would you be looking for help with those things from practitioners?

A: I hold the view that all there is, is truth. So everything — your fear, your desires, all of the ideas and theories about health and healing, and of course the bigger truths of our eternal essence — are all 100% true. The only question is how true, and perhaps more importantly how true for you right in this moment. It is 100% true that if you buy a lottery ticket you can win, but unfortunately it is not very true!

So your overwhelming desire to be done with the agony is completely natural, normal, and true. The question is, How true is that desire in this moment in your life? I often say that the truth is whatever opens your heart (or your awareness) and quiets your mind. Does your desire to be free of the pain open your heart and quiet your mind? Or does it close your heart and agitate your mind? There is no right or wrong answer, and it is always relative. It is possible that in some moments that desire closes your heart and in other moments it opens your heart. It depends on where you are to start with when the desire arises. Are you in the depths of apathy and despair? Then a desire to be somewhere else may be a bigger truth in that moment. Are you in a rare moment of acceptance or perhaps even just distracted by something else other than your agony? Then the desire may be a contraction of your heart, of your awareness in that moment.

The truth itself is big enough for all of the contradictions, and all of the different perspectives about who chooses and who or what you really are and how to live your life, and on and on and on. Even illusions are 100% truth, they just are not very big truths. An illusion is something real that appears to be something other than what it is. Trauma and conditioning are illusions, but that doesn't mean we don't ever have to deal with them. Ultimately, everything is an illusion, but nonetheless the illusions you are experiencing are here, and they are happening now. Seeing their illusory nature can help you move beyond them, but the point may not even be to move beyond all illusions, but to just get to know them so well that they don't trick you anymore. What are the illusions that are showing up here and now? How real or true do they seem, especially if you sense them with your heart? A good practitioner or healer can help with this uncovering or seeing through the illusion as they are naturally not as caught in the particular illusion you may be caught in, simply because it is not their illusion in that moment.

We don't always get to decide what truths we experience, but we can discriminate how true they are. For example, I've found that the idea that our thoughts cause our illness and suffering is often used as a judgment and so is usually not very true, as I have rarely found a judgment that opened my heart. However, if the idea is *not* being used to reject our experience or criticize someone, then it could still be a useful and even helpful or relevant piece of the truth. However, all ideas are only at best a small part of the truth. There is so much more going on in everyone including you than just your thoughts. How could they ever be the only cause of anything?

Everything you or I know about health and healing is also just part of the truth. So much always remains a mystery. Right now you do know what you are experiencing, and it sounds like it is beyond even my worst imagination of the worst that could happen to someone. But there is still so much that you and I both don't know. What is the ultimate effect of this much suffering on your soul? Can your soul be harmed, or does even the worst suffering eventually pass? Will your soul be much more wise and compassionate after this illness is over and long past? Is your soul much more wise and compassionate right now than when this illness started? Is it possible that, even if that compassion and wisdom is blocked most of the time by the pain, the compassion and wisdom are still here? Any conclusion even about these bigger questions that arises is just the conclusion in this moment. It is again a 100% true conclusion, but it is never the final conclusion. There is always the next conclusion and the one after that, and the conclusion after a couple hundred more lifetimes have gone by.

I am not sure that we are here to only make "better" choices. When I hold too tightly to the idea of something being "better" it tends to close my heart and sometimes even paralyzes me from making any choice. When I hold the idea of "better" lightly, then I make my choices and get on with it. Whatever comes of my choice is whatever comes of my choice, and my choice is only a very small part of what determines what comes next anyways. However, even though it is only a small part, it is still a part of what determines what comes next so I still try to make the "better" choice, I just don't worry too much about the results.

Similarly, when I have health problems which I have had my fair share of (although clearly much less than you), I just get curious about the choices that show up to be made, and do my best with them. Most of the time I experience it as something like wandering around in the dark. I try dozens of things that maybe help a little or maybe don't help at all. Then once in a blue moon, I experience something that seems to help a lot....at least for a while until the situation shifts again and suddenly it doesn't help anymore. In my best moments I find all of this fascinating and rich beyond words. In my worst moments I get caught in a small truth about how it should be, or what is wrong with me, or what is wrong with life that this should happen to me. The many experiences of very big truths that I have had do tend to make me relatively unconcerned when I get tangled up in a small truth. It seems like my over-arching lack of concern does mean that generally the small truths pass very quickly, but any effort on my part to get rid of them makes them stay a little longer. When I just accept them as being small, they usually pass very quickly.

So I seek treatment for my health issues, I just get on with my life, I get distracted by other things, I play with my dog, I sit and feel my way into the depths of presence and love, I eat lunch, I am swept up in awe, I am swept up in desire, I am lost in confusion, I experience a shatteringly profound insight, and on and on and on. All of this is life. All of this is truth. It is not up to me how big or how small a truth appears before me or arises from within me. I can resist, hold on, let go, laugh, cry and still the movement of life unfolds with more for me to be mystified by, and again, at my best moments, inspired to embrace and savor to the utmost.

I invite you to perhaps investigate until your head hurts from it and then do something else. Do everything you can to help yourself get better and then let yourself give up and do nothing. Take it all one moment at a time, and then worry like hell about the future and resent the past. Find something else to think about and then give up on that also. If you feel overwhelmed that is natural and normal given what you are experiencing. If somehow mysteriously in the deepest moments of agony there is a glimmer of acceptance and peace, that is also natural and normal. Sometimes the deepest surrender comes when we are way past the end of any rope. And sometimes more agony comes when we cannot believe there could even be any more agony.

I don't even know if anything is a big truth or a small truth, I only know what is here and how open or spacious my awareness is or how small and contracted it is in this very moment. The only constant is that I am very often surprised by what happens next, and even by where a bigger truth is actually found. Often it shows up in the center of the smallest truths I encounter. In that spirit, in this moment I send you as much light and love as I can imagine sending anyone. It might just touch you a little or it might reach deeply into the suffering you are experiencing. I hope maybe it is the latter, but I don't know what it means if in this moment you are touched. I just know it feels true to send the love your way in this particular and unique moment, and it touches me deeply to consider how difficult and overwhelming your situation is. I am humbled and saddened and mystified and broken open by compassion. And then to be honest and transparent about the unceasing movement of this mysterious thing called life, in a few moments, I will most likely just get on with the usual stuff and simply brush my teeth and go to sleep. But for now, you have my utmost love and compassion, as we truly are one and the same being. May you find all of the peace and ultimate healing that it is possible to find.

The Truth Is Not Necessarily Comfortable, It Is Just True

Q: I am a retired minister. Getting to where I now am has taken forty-five years. I'm terrified to publish my work or speak openly about what I now believe. I could be charged with heresy and stripped of my ordination. How does one deal with such a transformation in belief systems? What does one do with this? My answer for now is to just be, and when asked to preach or teach, to then translate.

A: I would suggest you listen to your heart. The truth is what opens your heart and quiets your mind. Does your fear open your heart? If fear closes your heart and constricts your awareness, then it simply isn't very true or very important. The things you fear might still happen, but so what? Since they are not actually very important, then just let them happen. Also, if your fears are not very true, then it is pretty unlikely that what you fear will happen.

All there is, is truth. So your fears are true, in that they *could* happen—they are just not very true. They could happen, but it might be very unlikely or very unimportant if they do happen. My favorite example of something that is true, but not very true is a lottery ticket. It's true that you could win but, unfortunately, not very true. In fact it is a ridiculously small truth. Even if you did win the lottery, it wouldn't matter that much, as there is not much truth in the imagined value of money or material possessions.

Listening to your heart can put all of this back into perspective. Following the truth that your heart shows you will not necessarily be successful, admired, financially rewarding, comfortable, or easy—although it could be. But it will be true, real, meaningful, deeply satisfying, and fulfilling. All of that is so much more important and true than anything your fears might be pointing to. It isn't very important what we think, what we feel, or even what we want. What matters is simply what is true.

A Tiny Paddle on the River of Life

Q: I would like to know whether thoughts create our reality. I think a lot of negative and fearful thoughts, which tend to become reality. So I want to know for sure whether it is true or is it just my assumption.

A: My sense is that thoughts do affect our experience but much less than we imagine. There are so many influences in every moment that affect what actually happens that, while thoughts do have an effect, it is not that much of an effect. The problem is that we tend to really notice the times when something we think about happens, and we overlook all of the times when we have had a negative or fearful thought and nothing ever came of it.

I invite you to test this out. For the next five days, take some time each day to write down twenty or so fearful or negative thoughts you have about the next day or so. Include anything that comes to mind. Then on the sixth day, go through the five lists of negative thoughts and check for yourself how many actually came true. Also note anything that happened, positive or negative, that was not on your lists.

Then, just to be thorough, for the next five days, write down twenty positive and hopeful thoughts about the next twenty-four hours. On the sixth day, go through the lists and see how many came true. Once again, note anything that happened, positive or negative, that was not on your lists.

This will show you how many of your thoughts come true. It might make it easier to stop giving so much attention to what you think when you find out how rarely your thoughts actually come true. Then you can become curious about what does actually happen, whether you thought about it or not. There is a deep and profound wisdom unfolding life, which is responsible for most of what happens. It moves through you and through everything in the world to affect what happens. Our thoughts can also affect this a little, but for the most part what is meant to happen will happen whether we think about it or not.

You might also reflect some on how you felt during the five days of writing down negative thoughts compared to the five days of writing down your positive thoughts. This may possibly be the main way your thoughts affect your experience: by changing how you feel as life unfolds. Having more positive thoughts probably won't change much about what happens, but you will feel better on those days.

As a final experiment, for five days, try writing down ten negative things and ten positive things, and then tear up the piece of paper and forget about them, and never check if any of them came true or not. Notice how you feel on the days when you don't give any importance to what you think will or won't happen. Does it feel better to have lots of positive thoughts or does it actually feel better to not pay attention to your thoughts at all?

A good metaphor is that in life we are in a small boat on a very large river. We are given a tiny paddle that we can use to move the boat this way and that way, but in the end, we are still going to go where the river is going. Similarly, your thoughts and even your choices are not likely to change the overall direction of your life in any profound way. You can paddle a lot, just a little, or not at all, and the river will still take you where it takes you. You may find it makes sense to pay more attention to the river and to the direction that life is already flowing than to your little thoughts that are like a tiny paddle.

Let me know how it goes for you if you try this little experiment.

Q: I tried the experiment with thinking negative and positive thoughts. I found that very few of the thoughts that I think actually come true in the short term. But I have the following doubts: The experiment works for short term thoughts, but what about deep underlying belief systems of fear, lack of self-esteem, and suspicion of people close to you. What I found is that these belief systems seem so overpowering when they are active that I am not able to let go of them. Why do they seem so solid and so difficult to overcome, when they are only thoughts?

A: Beliefs do seem to have a strong effect on our lives, but what is a belief other than a habitual thought, one that repeats often? Another aspect of having a habitual thought or belief is that it can operate unconsciously. It can run in the background, and it can also be present as an assumption within other thoughts that you consciously have. For example, an overall belief that life is dangerous is being assumed whenever you have a thought about what could go wrong or how you might get hurt.

This repetition, both conscious and unconscious, of a particular thought is what makes a belief seem so real and solid. Repetition gives the thought more apparent importance and weight. We are also strongly conditioned to think that our own thoughts are important and true. Notice how many times in an argument, someone says, "Well that's what I think!" as if that is all the evidence needed to prove their point! So when a thought habitually appears in our mind, it supports the illusion that it is somehow very true and real.

It is, as you say, still just a thought, but it is also a habit. The best approach to any habit that is not working for you is to create a new habit instead. It doesn't usually work to go to battle with an old habit, as that, paradoxically, reinforces it. But if you create a new habit instead and that becomes the new normal, then you are too busy with the new habit to do the old habit.

The steps to creating a new habit, including a new habit of belief (or a new habit of paying attention to something other than a thought or belief) are:

1. Become very curious about the old habit. You don't need to change it or try to get rid of it, but explore it enough to know how it works or doesn't work for you.

2. Invent a new habit or habits that work as well or better than the old habit. For example, if the old habit of fearful thoughts and beliefs was intended to protect you, find a new habit that also serves to protect you, such as becoming very aware of your surroundings and of what is happening in every moment. Being curious in this way would mean not focusing on what you *think* might happen but on what is actually happening. Along with protecting you better than the old habit, doing this will also make your life richer and more interesting. Alternately, you could come up with new, more positive beliefs to replace the old habitual beliefs, which is especially useful when the old beliefs are negative.

3. Spend at least 15-20 minutes a day practicing the new habit until it becomes established. Taking the previous example, spend 15-20 minutes a day repeating out loud the new positive beliefs, or spend that time being intensely curious about what is happening in the present moment. You can do this even more often if you like, especially at first. Even if you don't initially believe the new thoughts, say them out loud anyway. You don't need to try to believe them. Just think them out loud or write them down over and over again. A belief is just a thought you have repeated a lot, so you can turn positive thoughts into beliefs just by repeating them.

4. Continue practicing the new habit until it happens on its own and you notice that you are spontaneously thinking the new positive thoughts or being curious even when you aren't practicing being curious. The goal is to have the new habit be as automatic and unconscious as the old habit was. This transformation requires effort at first until the new habit becomes established.

In dealing with beliefs, be sure to include paying attention to something other than beliefs as one of the new habits, as in the example above of being curious about what's happening in each new moment. What else is here right now beside your thoughts, even your positive thoughts? There's a whole world of experience to explore beyond your thoughts and even beyond your body and senses. You can ask: What else is here besides my mind and body and also besides this entire world of form and objects. What about awareness itself? What happens when you create a new habit of paying attention to the space of awareness itself?

This is your life and your awareness. Why not spend your awareness—your attention—on things that serve you well and that you enjoy? If there is a habit of any kind that is limiting you, just create a new habit that works better. The best new habit is the habit of questioning, exploring, inquiring, discovering and uncovering all of the many dimensions of reality beyond our limited thoughts. Thoughts are not ever bad or wrong, but they are very small realities. After all, every thought you have ever had has fit between your ears, so how big can your thoughts be?! Reality is infinite, and most of it exists outside of the space between your ears, so why not make a habit of diving into and paying attention to all of reality?

Awareness Is "Me"

Everything is part of the whole truth. Every thought, expression, or experience contains some truth. However, a particular thought, expression, or experience can contain more or less truth than another thought, expression, or experience. It is your heart—your sense of yourself—that measures how true things are. Very simply, a larger truth opens or softens your heart or your sense of self. If you experience a smaller truth, then the sense of your self will be smaller or more contracted.

For example, if you think, "I'm separate from everyone and everything," notice how that affects your sense of self. Then compare that felt sense of self to the sense of self when you think, "I'm connected to everyone and everything " or "I'm one with everyone and everything." Just try out each thought. Which one feels truer? If it is harder to think one thought or the other, then just try it on like you'd try on a sweater or a costume. You don't have to "wear" either thought all of the time, but just try each thought on for size to see how true it is.

One day I noticed that it felt truer to say, "Awareness is me" than to say, "I am aware." It's not that it is untrue to say, "I am aware," but it simply opened my sense of self more to say "Awareness is me." What a difference that made to switch the subject and object in a sentence with the verb "to be" in it, which implies an equivalence or that one thing *is* the other. Saying "Awareness is me" seemed to emphasize "awareness" over "me," which feels truer. My heart softens and expands more with that statement than with "I am aware." It feels truer to notice how awareness is moving as this body, than to notice how this body is aware.

Don't just take my word for it, test it out for yourself. Take a moment to hold each of the following thoughts in your mind, and notice any difference in how large, open, expanded, or relatively smaller, tighter, or more contracted the sense of yourself becomes as you hold each thought:

I am aware.
Awareness is me.

You can also notice the effect of turning the object of the sentence into a verb. Which sentence feels truer?

I am aware.
I am "aware-ing. (i.e. I am doing this activity called awareness.)

Awareness is me.
Awareness is me-ing. (i.e. Awareness is doing this activity called me.)

You can also experiment with replacing the subject "I" with "awareness" in a number of other thoughts. Take a moment with each to notice which version of the sentence feels truer in your heart or sense of Being:

I am sitting here.
Awareness is sitting here.

I hear a bird singing.
Awareness hears a bird singing.
Or: Awareness is a bird singing.
Or: Awareness is singing.

I am my body. I have a body
Awareness is my body. Awareness has this body.

I like ice cream.
Awareness likes ice cream.

There is no wrong way to speak or think, and it might still make sense to say, "I like ice cream" in normal conversation. Fortunately, every sentence or thought contains some truth even if some sentences and thoughts are very small expressions of truth and so will naturally result in a relatively contracted and small sense of self. There is no right size for the sense of self, since the sense of self you're experiencing right now is always correctly showing you how true your thoughts or experiences are in this particular moment.

Nevertheless, you can play with the words and concepts to see how that affects your experience of Being in each moment. If you find a way of expressing experience that seems to capture more of the truth, then what a gift that is to feel your heart and sense of Being open in response. If you find that a habitual way of expressing the truth limits your experience of the truth, then why not try on some different thoughts for size? Maybe you will find a new array of thoughts, experiences, and even fundamental identities to add to your wardrobe!

What Is the Meaning of Life?

"What is the meaning of life?" is a wonderful question because it has no final or fixed answer. Meaning is a purely mental or conceptual experience, so it is always changing and evolving. This can mean that the question unfolds in new and ever-changing ways. It also suggests that if there is no final answer, there might also be a way to go beyond the question itself.

There is no inherent meaning in anything. We can squeeze an orange, and juice will come out, but no meaning will ever come flowing out with the juice. We can then add meaning to the experience: "I'm taking care of myself by eating healthy" or "What a treat to have fresh juice!" but the meaning that we gave to the juice is not an inherent quality of the juice itself.

Since there is no final answer to what the meaning of any experience or life itself is, the question can go on and on and unfold in myriad ways. At first, we might look for the meaning of life in what we are taught, in books or in our culture. We might conclude that the meaning of life is to get rich or to find your true love or to live a more spiritual life or some other idea we get from our families, schools, or media and culture. We can spend years pursuing the meaning of life in these ways. As a result, we are likely to discover that there are many different, and often contradictory, answers to this question.

When we first realize that there is not just one answer to this question, it can be a bit disorienting. What does it mean if what my parents or my culture taught me is not the only possible answer? But then we might discover that this open-ended quality to the question means that we can choose or create our own meanings in life. This opens the door to trying on lots of different perspectives. Today the meaning of my life may be about decorating my house, but tomorrow it may be about finding inner peace. The meaning of anything is simply a belief we hold in that moment, and all belief is actually make-believe. We get to make up our beliefs about life and everything in it.

Even then, the question is still there: What is the meaning of life now? And what about now? And what about the new moment that is happening now? This never-ending quality of the question points to an even deeper possibility: What would life be like without the question? Do we need to believe anything about life for life to happen, or does life unfold perfectly well when we have no ideas about it? How present are we to the actual reality of our life when we have an idea about what it means or is supposed to mean compared to when we have no preconceived notions about it? Does having an idea about the meaning of life always add to the experience, or does it sometimes get in the way of completely experiencing life as it is?

There is no right or wrong way to experience our beliefs about the meaning of life. We can accept what we are taught, we can explore myriad ways of perceiving and understanding life, or we can hold all beliefs so lightly that in a particular moment we have no ideas about life and are just here experiencing the raw aliveness of the moment.

One definition of truth is that the truth is whatever stops the questions. This stopping can be temporary, as when we decide that the meaning of our life is to pursue our career, and we get busy doing just that, and for a while forget about the question altogether. But again, "What is the meaning of life?" is such a powerful question because all of the answers are so temporary. Eventually, even a tremendously successful career is not enough, and the question comes back, and we get involved again with searching for or creating a new answer to the question.

Perhaps the closest we come to a final truth about the meaning of life is when we go beyond the search for a final answer and just live in this endless open-ended questioning with no answers, no ideas, no beliefs — just pure awareness, curiosity, joy, and wonder at all the experiences that life provides. Maybe the best answer to "What is the meaning of life?" is no answer at all. What is life itself like when we don't know the answers to any questions? What a strange and wonderful possibility — to use the deepest and most unanswerable questions to go beyond all questions.

The Gift of Self-Awareness

Q: What is the difference between awareness and attention? Something seems to still be aware of attention moving and zooming in and zooming out. You said awareness gets imprinted, and if the body walks out of a room, awareness follows it. What about the other people in the room? Are these different viewpoints of awareness, and is the whole of awareness attached to each body or how does that work? To say one is always only that space is fine enough, but it thinks it is the body, and then it gets painful. Until awareness wakes up to the fact that it is not the body, the life story is painful.

A: Here is how I experience it: awareness is a limitless, infinite presence. There is only one awareness, and it is already everywhere and every-when. It is the capacity to experience and be all of this world and everything in it. Its nature is also empty space, so it surrounds and permeates everything. Everything arises in awareness, and it doesn't pick or choose between experiences.

Since awareness already is everywhere, how can it move or change? Where would it go? So it came up with a simple solution: it moves within itself as attention. That way it can contract and focus and have all kinds of unique experiences within the larger field of its nature as pure presence. Attention is this movement within awareness. It doesn't harm or diminish awareness to contract, identify, and focus. That just creates a certain pressure or concentration of force within awareness that eventually dissipates again, like two scuba divers having a splashing fight thirty feet under the surface. They can push the water around and splash each other in the face, but in the end, the water is still the same.

So awareness contracts into a particular form or viewpoint and then experiences itself from this new perspective, as well as from other contracted perspectives (or bodies) in the same space. All life and all matter is an expression of this capacity that awareness or consciousness has to take on an apparent form and movement. To have a unique experience, awareness takes on the imprinting or conditioning of patterned focus and contraction. The human system is a particularly rich means for awareness to move within, and so it finds all kinds of unique ways to pay attention within the forms of multiple human minds and bodies.

Because the human body-mind is so good at paying attention and can even pay attention to itself, the possibility exists for both suffering and awakening. Suffering is what happens when we pay attention completely to the experience of our contracted sense of self and to what we think or want or fear. We become convinced that our thoughts about "me" and "my life" are not only real and true, but the whole truth and the whole reality of the moment. Our fears and desires become the totality of experience: "I want an ice cream cone, and if I don't get it, I can never be happy again!" What a powerful way to focus awareness, like a laser beam, on an ice cream cone!

Intensely focusing on thoughts, fears, and desires is the source of suffering, but being able to focus can also give us pleasure and joy, when we are focused on our senses, like when we are eating the ice cream cone. The ability to focus on, pay attention to, and identify with our desires, beliefs, sensations, experiences, opinions, fears, doubts, dreams, and wishes is not a mistake. For a long time in our human evolution, we experience great satisfaction in focusing our attention and fulfilling our desires. What a strange and glorious opportunity it is to be human and pay attention with such complete abandon and involvement and identification with whatever we focus on.

However, the human system also has a unique capacity to be self-aware. We can pay attention to our self and to awareness itself, since that is what we are made of. When the capacity to be self-aware arises, as a particular being evolves, there is a whole new possibility within this game of attention. When we first begin to pay attention to ourselves and reflect on our experience, we become aware of the tradeoff between pleasure and suffering. We realize that focusing on or paying attention to some things, such as desires and fears, has a price.

We notice that all this paying attention is both a source of enjoyment and the source of all of our suffering. What to do then? If we try not to suffer, that is just more trying and more suffering. But because we can notice the effects of our attention or, in other words, because we can pay attention to how we are paying attention, a completely new possibility arises: to simply choose to be aware of what is already here. We can pay attention to what is already in awareness. This is incredibly subtle and tricky at first: to catch the natural flow of awareness and join in with whatever it is already experiencing. It's like trying to sit exactly the way you are already sitting and breathe exactly the way you are already breathing and think whatever you are already thinking. All you add to any experience is noticing that you are already having that experience.

In one sense, we pay attention to awareness, but since awareness is like empty quality-less space, how do you do that? When you turn your attention back on awareness itself, you can get confused and disoriented because there is no thing called awareness, and attention needs an object to stay focused on. But you can catch a glimpse of the movement of awareness into attention by being curious about your attention. What's it like when you're paying attention to your thoughts? What's it like when you're paying attention to your desires? What's it like when you're paying attention to whatever appears in awareness in this very moment? I would suggest that you ask all of these questions of your body: What's it like in your body right now? Where is there sensation or tension? What is the underlying focus of that tension or sensation? Just be with the sensation in the body, and let it speak to you. What is it trying to experience or trying not to experience?

Becoming aware of that "trying" is all you need to do. Awareness, itself, can manage whatever comes from becoming aware of our trying or suffering. You can just bring awareness to the flow of attention, and then awareness will know what to do next. Often the contraction relaxes as more awareness flows within and around the previous focus. Sometimes the contraction will increase and give you an even clearer experience of contraction or identification. You can simply pay attention as if you were an "attention billionaire" and could never run out of attention. If you were a multibillionaire, you would probably realize that you no longer needed to think about where to spend or give your money. Well, you have a limitless supply of awareness, so there's no need to decide what to pay attention to and what not to pay attention to: just notice everything! When we pay attention to everything and anything, awakening is more likely to happen. At some point, we realize we are the limitless awareness, and not just this body or person. But no matter what, the pure flow of awareness is always here, even when we are intensely focused on only experiencing what we want to experience.

Q: I wanted to know whether we control where we are putting our attention, because it seems like even if we don't want to give our attention to thoughts, it automatically goes into thoughts.

A: I heard recently about some cutting edge new research into our brains, and it turns out there are two different functions in the brain: one is for concentration or focused attention and the second is a whole different set of neural pathways associated with a wandering, unfocused state of attention. Everyone has both of these capacities, and yet, we can develop or strengthen the part of our brain that can pay attention and focus. This is probably a big part of the benefit of meditation: it strengthens the part of our brain that can pay attention to whatever we choose to put our attention on.

As you may have discovered, even if you have meditated for years, at times your mind is still going to wander, and attention will be drawn to whatever thoughts happen to be occurring, which is normal. But we also always have the ability to focus or choose to pay attention to something else other than our thoughts. Even if we cannot stay 100% focused all of the time, we can develop or increase our ability to choose what we pay attention to and thereby increase the amount of time we are choosing what we pay attention to.

Perhaps if we develop this capacity more fully, then we could focus with less effort. We may even reach a point where no matter what we are doing with our attention, there is a relaxed sense of ease and effortlessness, similar to how a highly trained athlete can do amazing things effortlessly compared to an untrained or unfit person. Perhaps we can train ourselves to be able to more effortlessly focus attention and, therefore, not suffer as much. A well-trained athlete also trains his or her body to relax when effort is not needed, so perhaps we can train ourselves to not focus when that isn't necessary. The ideal may be a flexibility of focusing, which focuses when needed or when useful and relaxes whenever effortful or focused attention is not needed or useful.

It's fascinating when modern neuroscience supports ancient spiritual practices! This also points to how suffering is a very subtle phenomenon. When we are focusing on something pleasurable or interesting, that is not usually experienced as suffering, unless the effort to focus becomes extreme or obsessive. I often use the metaphor of a tight fist. If you make a fist and squeeze tightly, that isn't particularly painful or difficult. But if you squeeze extremely hard or hold the fist for several minutes, the effort involved can quickly become extremely painful. There is a similar effect when we struggle too hard to control any part of our experience, including the focus of our attention. It can be useful and appropriate to focus attention at times, but if we work too hard at it or become stuck in an obsessive loop of attention, then it can be a place of suffering.

Our awareness is not harmed even when we overly effort to focus it in a particular direction, just as usually our muscles are not permanently harmed when we overdo it in physical activity. The ideal may be to be able to flexibly effort and relax as needed. Life is rich, complex, and varied, so our response to it also needs to be rich, complex, and varied. What an amazing muscle awareness is! It can move in a truly astonishing range of dimensions of experience. Why not discover everything it is capable of, but also relax when life allows for a more open, spacious way of being aware?

Focusing Inward Through Self-Inquiry

At first, the spiritual practice of self-inquiry is just that: *IN*-quiry. It is turning our attention and curiosity inwards, towards the truth of our nature. It is a practice of redirecting attention away from objects, events, and experiences and towards the experiences within your body and being, including very subtle experiences. This inward focus can lead to an experience of your true nature and even beyond experience itself to a dimension that is empty of any experience or sense of self, to deeper realities that are beyond description.

The practice of inquiry can be quite simple. You begin by asking, "Who am I?" or "What am I?" or "What is here right now?" You can use any question that directs your attention to your sense of "me" or to your experience of existence. If your attention is flowing to an outer sensation or experience, you can ask, "To whom is this sensation or experience happening?" The obvious answer is that it is happening to "me." So then you ask again, "Who or what is this me?" Repeating these questions as each new experience or sense of me arises takes the experience more and more deeply into the inner aspects of your being.

When we explore what we call "me," we can find a lot of different aspects and even levels of experience that all seem to be "me" to some extent. There is a complex physical body and a wide range of physical sensations present here and now. There are thoughts, feelings, impulses, desires, intuitions, and subtler experiences happening all the time. All of these can seem like they are "me" or at least part of "me."

When we first ask, "Who or what am I?" we are likely to first notice our body. So the answer is simply, "I am this body." Or we might notice a particular aspect of the body, and so the answer might be, "I am a woman or man" or "I am 5 foot 8 inches tall" or "I am blond." Although these are fairly obvious and superficial answers, they are all correct and true. One bit of good news is that in doing inquiry, there are no wrong answers! Anything you can experience or notice about yourself is part of the truth of yourself.

If we notice the body or any aspect of the body, then we can inquire more deeply to discover more. One way to do this is to ask, "If I am more than this body (or a particular aspect of my body), then who or what am I?" Without making the first answer wrong or denying its truth, we simply ask, "What else is true? What else is here besides what I first noticed?" Whatever answer comes next, we ask again: "If I am more than that, who or what am I?"

We may find another answer that is a different aspect of our physical body or we might find an answer that is more subtle, which points to a different level of our experience of self. For example, we may say "I am a plumber" or "I am a spiritual seeker." These are not fixed qualities of our physical bodies but, rather, potential actions or functions of our whole being. Or we may notice an identity, capacity, emotion, belief, thought, or desire, and if we are identified with it, we will say, "I am depressed," "I am a success," "I am a funny guy," or "I am free." Again, there are no wrong answers, but you can then ask: "If I am more than that, what am I?"

Deeper and More Subtle Levels

Asking these questions naturally uncovers deeper and more subtle levels of our being. While at first, you might find that the answers relate a lot to your physical nature and the bundle of thoughts, identities, capacities, actions, feelings, desires, habits, and conditioning that make up what we call the individual, after a while, you might find that the answers that come relate to more essential aspects of your nature. You may have a sense in that moment that you are the peace, joy, love, compassion, or any of the more essential qualities that underlie our superficial nature. And yet, even when you uncover a deeper truth, you can always still ask, "If I am even more than infinite peace, then who or what am I?"

As the process unfolds, you may move more deeply into the truth of your being. You might experience a very fundamental quality of all Being such as awareness, empty spaciousness, or oneness. These are qualities of everything throughout eternity. Everywhere you go, there is space, everything that exists has some consciousness or awareness, and everything is connected and actually one thing or one Being. When your inquiry uncovers a fundamental quality of existence, that is just another dimension to be discovered, and you can still inquire further: "If I am more than pure awareness, what am I?"

The deeper and more subtle layers that get uncovered have more reality and impact on your being, especially when you first uncover them, than the more superficial layers of the body, mind, and personality. So even though they are not physical or solid in the usual sense, they are more real and substantial. This becomes obvious anytime you experience your essence or the fundamental qualities of existence itself.

The impact of the experience is beyond anything that you can experience in the more relative levels of your existence.

These more fundamental levels are also simply bigger. True peace and joy are infinite. Space has no limits. Pure awareness or consciousness is eternal. As a result, when your inquiry uncovers such a vast dimension of your true nature, it no longer really makes sense to call it "me." The words "I" and "me" just don't compute when you experience yourself as all space and all time. It can help at these points in the process to allow the questions to become more open-ended and undefined. For instance, it might make more sense to ask questions such as, "What boundaries are there to peace?" "What is here right now?" "What is happening now?" "What is true about awareness in this moment?" or to just hold an open questioning attention that takes in as much of what is present as possible with no words needed. Obviously, an indefinable wordless experience of limitless true nature is a very valid discovery when doing inquiry!

Inquiry can lead to moments where all of our usual concepts and experiences are no longer relevant and the world and our entire sense of self can dissolve completely. There is no way to really describe this kind of nonexperience in words, but it is a possible result of going deeper and deeper with more and more open-ended inquiry.

Maps of Reality and the Purpose of Inquiry

The examples I am using imply a certain map of reality and of the truth of our nature. There are many such maps, including highly detailed and complex maps, such as the map provided by the Diamond Approach as developed by Hameed Ali (aka A.H. Almaas). Students of the Diamond

Approach spend years exploring the many qualities of essence and different dimensions of Being that have been mapped out in the body of knowledge about true nature within that particular school or teaching.

In contrast, there are very simple maps such as the ones offered by some of the more purist Advaita or nondual teachings. In some of those maps, there are only two "locations": all appearances and experiences, which are seen as illusory and unimportant, and the ultimate reality of one pure consciousness in which everything else appears and disappears. This kind of map can be helpful at times in cutting through all the layers to the deepest reality. However, it can also be limiting if inquiry lands someone in one of the more relative levels and there is a rejection of or denial of the more relative truth. Again, there are no wrong answers, so it can be helpful to have a more complete map at times when you arrive in some unfamiliar dimension of your being that nonetheless is a powerful and liberating experience, even if it is not the ultimate truth.

This raises the question of what is the purpose of inquiry. In some traditions, the sole purpose of inquiry is to take someone to the deepest realization of no-self or emptiness that is possible. And in other traditions, the purpose of inquiry is to become familiar with and explore all the different dimensions of reality, including the deepest reality. In this broader view of the journey of inquiry, the ultimate is not any particular experience or nonexperience. The ultimate is complete and total flexibility to experience and even function within all of reality's many expressions. Again this flexibility is only complete if it includes the deepest realizations of emptiness and beyond. But it would seem that a complete perspective would not create a new, more subtle duality between true nature and the many levels of existence, including ordinary everyday identity as a particular individual. Everything and every possible experience is part of the totality of existence and is therefore a potential discovery as a result of inquiry.

Perhaps just as there are no wrong answers to the inquiry questions themselves, there is no right or wrong overall purpose to inquiry. Whatever results you pursue or stumble upon in doing inquiry are there to be discovered, and since nothing is ever finished within eternity, who knows where life and inquiry and awareness will take you next!

Practical Pointers

Here are a few more practical pointers for doing inquiry:

1. As mentioned briefly, there is another form of the questions that can be used as the process unfolds. Whatever answer or experience or even distraction comes in response to the question, "Who am I?" is then further explored with a question such as: "To whom or to what does this experience or answer arise?" or "Who or what is having this experience?" or "Who or what arrived at this answer?" The obvious answer is "me." "I am having this experience" or "I came up with this answer." So then you can return to the original question, "Who or what am I?" This cycle of alternating questions can take you deeper and deeper into your direct present moment experience of being, just as when using the follow up question of "If I am more than that, who or what am I?"

2. As the process unfolds, you can get very creative with the questions, since the questions are not the important thing (there are more at the end of this essay). The important thing is directing awareness or attention to aspects of your own experience that have not been consciously realized yet. For most people, this initially means directing attention inward to more subtle aspects of your individual experience. But as you reach the more universal dimensions of being that are also found within your individual experience, you may notice that it no longer matters what direction your inquiry is directed. It is just as rich and mysterious to inquire deeply into any object, experience, activity, or phenomenon as it is to inquire within. At that point, really any question will serve. Or you can just explore with a open curiosity using words when it seems appropriate in the moment and dropping all words when they are not really needed to direct attention to the mysteries all around you and everywhere within you. For example, it can be fun to strip the question down to "Am I?" or even more to "Am?" which in essence is asking "Does anything exist?" This question points to the simple fact that you *are*, regardless of what you are experiencing. Beneath everything that's going on, is a sense of existing. This form of the self-inquiry question points to a dimension other than experience.

Once that sense of existence is in your field of awareness, then it's possible to find out what's true about your existence, to explore that. What's it like right now to just be? Is it enough right now to just exist? Or is there a sense that it's not enough? All our lives we've been told it's not enough: You have to be smarter, richer, prettier, more enlightened, more compassionate, more loving, and on and on. You have to be some *thing*.

We have the sense that if we could just *be* what we're supposed to be, then we could just be. Take a fantasy about being richer, for instance: What's great about being richer is that you think it will finally allow you to just be because you no longer have to become richer. We think that being richer or smarter will finally allow just being to be enough. Wherever this inquiry takes you, it's amazing to discover both the extent to which our existence is enough and the extent to which we think it isn't.

For most, this sense of existing is associated with the body. Existing seems to happen there. However, does your sense of existence stop where your body stops? Discover for yourself where your experience of *I am* is right now. Is it in the body or is the body in it? Would it be more accurate to say "I exist in the body" or "the body exists in *me*"? Be willing to hold the possibility that who you are goes beyond the body even if you aren't experiencing that directly right now. The experience of the body never goes away, but the link between the *me* and the body can soften or dissolve when "I am the body" is seen as only part of the truth. If you experience the *me* outside the body even a little, then the body can't be the whole truth of who you are.

Where does your sense of *me* stop? Right now, for instance, allow more of your experience of the room into awareness. When you include in your awareness the energy and information that's flowing in and out of the body, is there a greater or lesser sense of *me*? What is more true, to say, "I exist in this room" or "this room exists in me"? When you include the totality of the room and beyond, are you more in contact with your sense of your true self or less in contact with it? Most people find that the more they include in their experience, the larger their sense of me. When you ask these self inquiry questions, you discover there's not such a clear-cut boundary to me.

Of course, this exploration doesn't have to stop with your body or with this room. Try sensing the reality of the surrounding city. Is there a greater or lesser sense of *me* when you do this? You can also ask the question: Do I exist in space or does all of space exist in me? Which feels truer?

3. As the inquiry moves deeper, a common experience is emptiness. This can be a kind of relative emptiness, where the relative absence of something is experienced. For example, there may be a flatness or lack of joy or meaning. Or you may feel a mental emptiness that seems like confusion or blankness in the mind. Often, underneath our more superficial experiences of emotions or desires, there is an inner sense of something lacking or missing. When we are sad or hurting there may be an underlying sense of a lack of compassion or tenderness. When we are angry, there may be an underlying sense of weakness or lack of strength.

These relative experiences of emptiness or lack are often interpreted by the mind as mistakes or a sign that our inquiry is going in the wrong direction, like when you're looking for your car keys and you open a drawer that's empty and you immediately conclude that's the wrong place to look, and so you open a different drawer. However, the inner experiences of emptiness or lack that we encounter during inquiry are actually tremendous opportunities to take the inquiry deeper. The experience of emptiness or lack is often the most open doorway to the next level or layer of our being. Paradoxically, the place where we feel a lack of love is often the place where a deeper, truer experience of essential love will most easily be uncovered. The place where we feel the weakest is where true strength can be uncovered, and so on.

So when your inquiry brings you to a dry, empty, lacking place with no juice or excitement, instead of turning away, that is an opportunity to sense more deeply into that experience to find out what is present in the empty space.

This principle of emptiness being an open doorway applies at every level of inquiry. When a profoundly empty experience of no-self is uncovered, you can savor that pure spacious emptiness, and yet you can also become curious as to what lies beyond even that utter blankness of no-self or no-experience. What is present even when there is no self? Perhaps whatever we might conceive of as the ultimate truth is itself just another doorway into even greater mysteries.

4. Another way to ask the self-inquiry questions is with your whole heart. You ask them with everything you've got, as if your life depended on it. If you ask a self-inquiry question with this kind of passion and intensity, it will bring you beyond what the mind is able to figure out. When you ask it with your whole heart and you don't find an answer, you just stay there, not knowing. You just let yourself not know. There's nothing but that space, and you just stay present to that space, to that sense of there being nothing behind your eyes, nothing behind your thoughts, nothing behind your feelings. Instead of turning back to thing-ness when you don't find anything, you just stay there in the no-thing-ness and get curious about it. Nothing—what's that like?

In looking and finding nothing, what you discover is even more space. Staying with the self-inquiry question, "Who am I?" opens up space. Nothingness is very spacious; there's a lot of room in it. When you stay in that nothingness, you discover that there's a lot of stuff in that space, stuff that is real in a way that the stuff in the world has never been real. What moves in that space are true qualities of Being, such as love, compassion, insight, and strength.

Every time you turn towards Beingness, a different quality shows up. Being has an infinite number of qualities, which show up fresh and different in every moment. These qualities can seem to exist in another dimension, as they have a depth and solidity about them that is more real than physical objects.

5. It is possible to do this inquiry alone by asking yourself the questions or in a dyad, where one person asks a question and another person answers. Then the first person asks a question again, and so on. After a while you can switch roles. This way of doing inquiry is especially powerful, as it keeps you focused on the process and doesn't allow your mind to wander.

If you are doing it alone, and it is appropriate to do so, it can also help to speak the questions and answers out loud. Doing inquiry out loud involves your entire brain. The words go out your mouth and then go back in both ears, which engages both hemispheres of the brain.

6. I will leave you again with the most important pointer of all: there are no wrong answers or wrong experiences when doing inquiry. We are not in control of what arises when we do inquiry, but there is an infinite intelligence unfolding everything in life, and it knows exactly what experience, insight, or understanding is needed in this and every moment. When you practice formal inquiry or anytime you are simply curious about life and awareness and existence,

wherever that process takes you in the moment is exactly where you need to be. Inquiry will sometimes lead us to dive deeply into the ultimate mysteries and then, in the very next breath, uncover an intensely contracted piece of our conditioning. What an opportunity that is to see the truth of that experience! Who knows what new and unexpected doorway into essence and what new undiscovered dimensions of Being are hiding in the place where our deepest wounding is stored!

This journey of inquiry is the ultimate rollercoaster ride, which includes the highest highs and the lowest lows. It is all worthy of our fullest curiosity and of our fullest devotion and love.

Suggestions for Some More Questions to Use in Self-Inquiry

- Who are you? What are you? If you are more than that, then who or what are you? Who or what are you right now, in this moment? If you are more than that, who or what are you? Keep repeating.

- Who or what is experiencing that thought, feeling, sensation, spaciousness etc.? Who or what is experiencing that feeling? Who or what is experiencing that sensation? Who or what is seeing? Who or what is hearing? Who or what is noticing that?

- Who or what is this I? (If the answer is "I" am experiencing the sensation).

- What am I aware of right now? You may answer with an "I" statement, stating something you are aware of: "I'm aware of x. I'm aware of y." Who or what is the "I" that is aware? (pause) Is there an I that is aware?

- Experiment with replacing "I" with "Awareness" in your answers. For example, "Awareness is hearing the bird singing." "Awareness is noticing the plant." "Awareness is sitting in the chair."

- Notice what is noticing (What is aware? What is experiencing?). What is that? What is that like?

- Are you aware right now? What's that like?

- Who or what is aware? Can you find what is aware? Where is it located? Who or what is experiencing Awareness? (Answer: me, your name) Where is (your name)? Is Awareness in you or are you in Awareness? Can you find yourself in Awareness?

- Can you find a boundary between you and Awareness? Where does (your name) leave off and Awareness begin?

- What is the source of Awareness? To discover the source of Awareness: Notice the plant or something else in your environment. Now notice where you noticed that from. Where do you notice the source of noticing from? Then where did you notice that noticing from?

- What else is here right now besides a thought, feeling, sensation, space, etc.? What is prior to that?

- What is speaking these words in this moment?

- What is listening? What is seeing? What is sensing, What is thinking?

- What knows that?

- What else are you experiencing now?

- Where's the boundary between x and y? For example, between a thought and the space it's occurring in, or between words and the space they're appearing in, or between the sense of yourself and the Silence?

General Instructions for Doing Inquiry as a Dyad

Take turns asking the questions and answering them. It is best if one person just asks for a while and then you switch roles so that the person answering can go deeply into the process of answering. There is no right or wrong answer to the questions posed by the questioner. The question is a pointer, pointing the person to true nature. The person asking the questions should allow the person to take as much time as he or she needs to formulate an answer, and then follow up everything the answerer says with a related question. If someone doesn't have an answer or cannot speak the answer, he or she can simply say "pass," and then the questioner can follow up with a new question. The questions ideally keep pointing deeper and deeper to the source of awareness itself. Relax and have fun with the process!

Just As It Is

Q: Over the last five months or so, I've diligently practiced self-inquiry. The fruits of the practice were extremely beneficial, as I felt a deep, luminous peace in the so-called heart center by drawing the mind inward via this inquiry. But lately, I feel I've hit a barrier. How can this problem be solved?

A: These ups and downs and fluctuations are quite normal, and everything is unfolding perfectly. However, here are a couple of suggestions:

Explore different ways of doing the inquiry. You can also use this experience itself as a new direction for the inquiry by sensing deeply into the felt sense of the barrier and exploring it as fully as you can. Especially explore the sense of self that the barrier gives you and also the sense of self that any resistance you might feel to the barrier gives you.

Alternatively, just let go of the inquiry for a while and either return to your meditation practice or try a completely new spiritual practice. The body-mind naturally becomes acclimated to any repetitive activity, so it can be helpful to change your approach occasionally. After a while, you can return to the inquiry and see if you have a different result. You may find a new and richer appreciation for it after you've been away from it for a while.

Finally, remember that all spiritual practice is just a way of making yourself available to Grace. Whatever you experience and whatever results appear are completely up to the infinite intelligence that is and always has been unfolding your life. Your experience in every moment is guided and created by that intelligence. Even this barrier you feel is here for a very good reason. There is no wrong experience to inquire into; it is all grist for the mill. What is the gift that the barrier is giving you? What is it showing you that you have not seen yet? And what is here right now that is completely untouched by, and at peace with, the barrier just as it is?

Forgiving Our Human Failings

Years ago, I read something by Satyam Nadeen, where he suggested that prior to his spiritual awakening, his conditioning (specifically his Enneatype as described by the Enneagram) could clearly predict 90% of his behavior. That left 10% of the time when he was acting in a more spontaneous and authentic way. After his awakening, he found that his conditioning still seemed to determine 80% of his actions, and so that meant that now 20% of the time he was being more authentic and responding in the moment.

Those numbers are probably not very exact, and every person's experience would be unique in the degree to which their conditioning was transformed. But it is striking in a number of ways that the change he observed in himself was not as radical and total as some might expect from a profound spiritual awakening.

A lot of our conditioning is not actually problematic, so it is likely that much of it would not change. There are lots of practical aspects to our programming, ranging from knowing how to change a flat tire to subtle appropriate social behaviors that are generally useful and functional in daily life. It seems reasonable that many of these kinds of conditioned behaviors might not be affected much at all by a deep recognition of our true underlying nature. This is like software on our computer that works well for what it is intended to do.

The rest of our conditioning has a tremendous amount of momentum, and so it is still not surprising that even some of the less functional aspects of our conditioning might not be instantly dissolved in even a series of spiritual realizations. Perhaps this can help in understanding why even great spiritual teachers have at times behaved in less than ideal ways. Even when a great deal of conditioning has been dissolved, there are bound to still be pockets of dysfunctional patterns in every human being.

An opportunity in all of this is to have compassion and forgiveness when someone we admire acts with less integrity. If we hold someone to an unrealistic standard of perfection, we are bound to be disappointed.

There is a flip side to this: 20% authenticity is double the amount of spontaneous and genuine action compared to someone who is still only able to access deeper sources of inspiration and motivation 10% of the time. The reason we are so drawn to spiritual leaders as role models is that, in comparison to the average person, there is a refreshing and inspiring amount of genuine authenticity that is undeniably present. We can still appreciate and honor the wisdom, kindness, presence, and love that flow more abundantly in a person who has a profound degree of spiritual development.

In every relationship, whether it is with a teacher, a friend, a family member, or even with ourselves, we can still be discriminating enough to recognize when actions are authentic and coming from an essential aspect of Being or when they are coming from a more conditioned and limited aspect of our nature. The latter is almost always an opportunity to hold someone with compassion and forgiveness, even as we take appropriate action to protect ourselves or others if necessary.

It helps to keep things in perspective: What is the whole truth of the relationship or of our own actions? Perhaps by understanding that even a high degree of spiritual insight and awareness doesn't mean someone is 100% beyond reproach, we can learn to not throw the baby out with the bathwater, but also to not drink the bathwater just because the baby is so cute. The balanced view is to see the human and the Divine, the conditioned actions and the relative gifts of freedom and authenticity, and to respond when appropriate to the whole person.

I have found that in every human relationship I have had (including those with my spiritual teachers and spiritual friends), there has always been a mix of enlightened action and conditioned reactivity. I find the same mix in my own behavior, and while I still question and examine my own actions and those of others, I mostly find that acceptance and understanding is the most useful response. In accepting and forgiving the limitations in myself and in the very human friends and teachers I have known, I am able to also benefit most profoundly from their sometimes remarkable and inspiring holiness.

Acceptance and forgiveness is also the most effective way to bring transformation to our own conditioning and the conditioning of others. Of course, it is always appropriate to take action to protect yourself and others from physical or emotional harm. Being forgiving doesn't imply allowing truly unhealthy behavior to continue. But compassion and forgiveness is the path forward when we encounter the remaining pockets of painful conditioning in ourselves and in our dearest friends and guides.

In the deepest sense, forgiveness is seeing the whole truth. We naturally forgive even a very unkind person when we see that it is not their true nature that is being unkind, just as it is not the true nature of a spiritual master who occasionally acts without kindness. Unkindness always flows from the conditioning that we have accumulated in this and possibly many lifetimes. This conditioning is not our fault. We did not put it there, and it naturally takes time for it to be completely resolved.

If we understand that behavior is always a mixture of the divine and the conditioned as long as we are human, then forgiveness and acceptance is a natural response. In the challenging interplay of human interactions, it helps to remember that love is for giving and love is forgiving.

Gratitude and Acceptance Can't Hurt!

Q: I have recently come to realize that we must be grateful for everything, including all situations and circumstances that are presented to us, not just those we find pleasant and somehow self-benefiting. I have been taught that expressing gratitude for something in my life communicates to the Universe that I want more of this. How does one bring an end to suffering and pain even as one is expressing gratitude for this same suffering and pain?

A: Just as if you had a broken bone, you would see a doctor and get a cast, if there is something that you can do to reduce suffering and pain, it makes sense to do it. At the same time, acceptance of and even gratitude for the challenges and limitations of life can reduce or eliminate the suffering even if the pain or limitation is not resolved, because most suffering is actually caused by the mental activity of resistance and rejection. The thought that something is wrong or should not be happening is often responsible for more pain and suffering than the actual circumstances.

Approaching difficulty with gratitude can be profoundly transformative on many levels and, surprisingly, can even allow a clearer seeing of the difficulty, which may make a practical solution easier to discover or carry out. The less we are creating suffering around our circumstances by what we are thinking, the easier it is to be present and curious and perhaps discover a solution. And if there is no solution, then gratitude and acceptance can't hurt! It feels good to be open and accepting, so why not feel as good as you can, given the circumstances?

Why not do everything you can to make a situation better and, at the same time, approach it with as much acceptance and gratitude as you can? Even when it is hard or impossible in a particular moment to accept or feel grateful, it is still possible to accept that you cannot accept the situation. This is the trick to accepting when it is hard: start with what you can accept or feel grateful for. Often if you accept that you are not feeling any gratitude or acceptance, this primes the pump and gives some momentum to acceptance. Doing this might be easier than trying to accept the bigger situation.

Conversely, being grateful for an unpleasant or unwanted situation can open up the flow of acceptance to include the simple reality that you don't want or like the situation. If you accept and are grateful for your own preferences, then you can still be letting life and other people know what you want more of and what you want less of without having to shut down the gratitude for however it does happen to turn out eventually. Gratitude and desire are not contradictory, they are complementary. Gratitude happens to be a bigger or fuller expression of our true nature, and so when that is present, our desires are seen to not be as important. But they can still be here, and you can even be grateful for the desires themselves. You can pursue your desires and yet also be just as grateful when you don't get what you want as when you do.

The mind tends to see opposites as contradictory: "If I am truly accepting, then I can't fix the problem." But we can both accept *and* fix, feel gratitude *and* make improvements, let the universe know what we like and don't like and also be filled with joy no matter what actually happens.

Egos Are Like Fruit Flies!

Q: I am having the fear of dying arise. I see facing this fear as a significant step, possibly even the biggest step, in moving beyond acting from my ego. Do you have any advice about this?

A: As for death, I will share an anecdote. When I was about 20, I went into a deep depression and wanted to escape life by dying. Then I started having a series of out of body experiences that were vivid and powerful. At one point, I suddenly and deeply realized that essentially nothing would change if I died. Whatever difficulties or problems I was experiencing would still be there wherever I landed after dying. Paradoxically, instead of overwhelming me, this realization freed me. I figured if there truly was no escape, I might as well enjoy myself. And that is what I did. Within just a few months, I went on a skiing vacation to Colorado, went back to school to study alternative energy, and got a great job as a solar energy system designer and installer. That deep sense that death doesn't matter one way or the other has stayed with me ever since.

Death, whether of the body or of the ego, is not very real or important. When the ego dissolves, life is still pretty much the same. Just as we can form a new body (either physical or subtle), we can reform a new ego in a heartbeat. In fact, everyone's ego "dies" several times a day. It is pretty easy to kill a thought-stream, and that is all the ego ever really is. When we pause our thinking for a minute, the ego that was there disappears. The fear of death, like most fears, is based on a misconception that there is something lost when we die. What can be lost was never real to start with, including the self of past lives, the ego you had this morning before breakfast, and the ego after that, and so on.

Egos are like fruit flies that hatch, breed and die in a few moments! When you realize the extremely transient nature of our ego identities and fears, they may still arise, but they are seen to not be important or meaningful. You can just wave the ego flies away and bite into the fruit of life itself. Or you can be curious about the flies if you find them interesting. What a mystery it all is, including the most temporary and brief experiences in life.

Q: If it's like what you describe, what a bleak picture: learning our lessons with such painful slowness, taking on an ego again, which can only be seen through by means of suffering, and on a mundane level having to learn to wear diapers, walk, and go through adolescence again! The teaching, "death is just merging back into where you came from" is supposed to remove our fear of death, but in my view it completely misses the point. The greater fear is of having to start all this over again.

A: Our worldly life is a schoolhouse. The way you master the lessons of life is to accept and embrace them totally. If you get in the habit of loving every little experience that comes along, then the big glimpses are just one more opportunity to open and allow everything. If you cannot accept and embrace what is happening, then in that moment you are in a place of suffering and the lesson is delayed and has to be repeated.

At every twist and turn, the most important question is, Can I accept and even embrace this experience as it is? If the answer is no, that is not really a problem, as then the question becomes more subtle: Can I accept and embrace that I cannot accept and embrace this moment? If you are in resistance or judgment, then you are in resistance and judgment. If you can see this clearly and fully accept and embrace that you are suffering from your resistance and judgment in that moment, then paradoxically, you are back in a place of acceptance and can even learn from your experience of resistance. Strangely, suffering is no longer suffering when we embrace it. Once you are in a place of acceptance of your resistance, it sometimes becomes more possible to also accept the thing you were resisting in the first place.

Our conditioning to resist any suffering is strong, so it can take a while to get the hang of embracing your suffering. We tend to suffer over the fact that we are suffering! But the reward for accepting your resistance is that you no longer are suffering at any moment when you turn towards what is here right this very instant, even if the experience right now is one of resistance and suffering. Even the fear of having to come back and experience this human life is no longer a problem if you can simply accept fully that you are afraid.

Is fear really a bad experience? What are the sensations we call fear? Are they bad sensations or just particular sensations? Is there any part of you that is actually enjoying the drama and intensity of fear while it is happening? And if you cannot embrace your fear as it is happening, can you embrace your resistance or judgment of fear? Is there any part of you that is already enjoying the resistance and judgments you may have about even your deepest fears?

It truly is all grist for the mill. And paradoxically when you can enjoy and accept every moment of fear, doubt, resistance, worry, judgment, desire, stuckness, shame, contraction, overwhelm, confusion, loss, despair, pain, and even physical death and also every moment of joy, pleasure, bliss, satisfaction, clarity, love, peace, expansion, acceptance, surrender, awakening, and liberation, then it no longer matters if you come back for a million more lifetimes. It is all fundamentally the same, and it is all rich and worthwhile.

Of course, the ultimate paradox is that when it is completely okay to come back a million more times, you probably won't. But the freedom is when it doesn't matter either way. Then if by chance you are meant to be a kind of bodhisattva and stick around a while longer to help other beings on their journey, so be it. And if you are simply meant to move onto the next adventure in consciousness, so be it. Slow is just slow and fast is just fast. The biggest freedom never looks like we expect it to, but it is totally free.

Commitment vs. Spontaneity: Why Not Both?

Q: I have an issue with commitment, especially when it comes to my work. I am very creative and I have lots of new ideas all the time, which sway me from one sphere of life to another. For example, I committed to investing my time in meditation and spiritual work for the next two years, but then I missed my art and writing, so I went back to writing. Then I talked to someone about my purpose in life, which he told me was to instruct people spiritually through creativity and art, so now I find myself going in that direction. I find it so confusing. I really love listening to what is right for every moment, but then I'm afraid I might go off track and not get anywhere. Sometimes I just find myself enjoying sitting and feeling the freedom of doing nothing.

A: The opportunity is to really be with the questions: What is the role of commitment? What am I committed to? When do I follow my commitments, and when do I follow my more spontaneous impulses? How are both of those experiences enriching me and how are they limiting me?

There are no right or wrong answers, and the answers do naturally and continuously change and evolve. Sometimes the best answer is "all of the above." You might want to explore how you can express both commitment and spontaneity in your daily life. There is room here for both of these approaches to living. They are complementary, not contradictory. There is a richness that is added to our commitments when we hold them lightly and allow spontaneous actions and impulses. And there is a richness that is added to our spontaneity when we hold more firmly at times to our deeper commitments. When musicians improvise, they often start with some kind of structure or melody, or else the improvisation can be scattered and uninteresting. A little structure can paradoxically free the improvisation to really soar and spread its wings.

The biggest truth is that it doesn't matter that much where you get to or what you accomplish in life, since the most important thing is what you already are and have always been: pure aware presence. And yet, this bigger truth can actually free you to try many different ways of living and acting on the more relative level. If it doesn't matter that much what you accomplish, you are free to make and keep commitments sometimes. You are also free to change and move more impulsively sometimes. You can even explore the possibility of being both committed and spontaneous simultaneously.

Why not include all of the activities you mentioned in your daily life at various moments? And of course, you can include just sitting and doing nothing. That is immensely valuable in itself. If you include all of the possible activities over time, then maybe instead of getting somewhere, you will get everywhere! You are infinite and eternal, so you can take your time and do it all!

I will add that the real value of commitment is not in the future. The real value of commitment in relationships and our work is that it can paradoxically free us to be more in the present moment. If you are committed to your lover, then you can set aside for this moment the questioning of whether to be in the relationship or not, and just be here now with your lover in both difficult and pleasant moments. No one knows what the future will actually bring, but right now, what are you committed to? How does that commitment enrich your life in this moment? Does holding back from commitment actually limit you in this moment from being your fully spontaneous and authentic self? It can work both ways. If a commitment frees you to be more in the moment, then it is worthwhile and worth holding on to. If over time, you discover that a commitment mostly interferes with the fullest expression of your authentic self, then it is appropriate to re-evaluate that commitment.

Both commitment and spontaneity are spiritual muscles that are worth strengthening. A full, rich, complete exploration of life requires both abilities. And while it can be humbling at times to look at yourself with clear-eyed discrimination, you may already have a sense of which "muscle" is already strong in your individual expression and which "muscle" could use some more exercise. In balancing your life, you can celebrate the abilities you already have developed and then also experiment with the other possible ways of more fully living your life.

Silence vs. Satsang

Q: I attended many gatherings for satsang in the last few years. It's too noisy. I like silence more. But it confuses me, because it is said that there's power in doing things together with others. Can you please explain the dichotomy? How can I pursue and start enjoying silence more?

A: There is no formula that works for everyone. If you are drawn to silence, then trust your inner sense of things. At some point that might also shift, and you may feel drawn again to more contact with groups. It is natural to sometimes find interactions with others too noisy, as you say. Your own heart and your deepest sense of what feels true for you is the best guide.

There is no real dichotomy here, since all spiritual practices are complementary, not contradictory. The art is to explore them with openness and curiosity. If a spiritual practice or activity is meant for you at a particular time, it will resonate with you and have a beneficial effect. If it is not meant for you at a particular time, you will feel contracted or stirred up by the practice, or it will simply have little or no effect on you. So while it can be worthwhile to explore a range of practices and approaches, the best way to measure their appropriateness for you at a particular time is to notice their effect on you. This should be clear within a week or two after starting any practice.

As for silence itself, outer silence is the simplest way to experience more inner silence. So anytime you sit still and just breathe or listen to the more subtle sounds of your body or of nature, that can naturally evoke more silence.

However, there can be a kind of "noisy" silence, where you sit quietly, but your mind is very busy and loud. That is also normal and natural. Often if you just continue to sit quietly, the mental noise will quiet down. Making space for the mind to quiet in this way is a big part of what meditation is all about. Recent research in neuroscience has suggested that the process of quieting the mind can take forty-five minutes or more. So if you can meditate for an hour or longer at a time, you may find that the results of your meditation are more effective.

Aspects of our conditioning or mental thought patterns often cause much of the excess mind activity. This is where a practice of inquiry can be helpful in loosening and eventually releasing some of the stickier conditioning we have accumulated. Any deep questioning and curiosity about your thoughts, experiences, and identifications can begin to unravel them. You can do this inquiry on your own or with a guide, either in a group setting, such as satsang, or in one-on-one mentoring sessions with a teacher.

The Real Cause of Suffering

A friend wrote me an email sharing how after a period grooving along in a place of gratitude and acceptance, he experienced an extremely painful and debilitating cerebral hemorrhage that left him unable to do most activities even after six months of rehab. He shared that he lives in fear every day of the hemorrhage reoccurring, and asked if I had any wisdom to share. Here is what I wrote in reply:

The real cause of suffering is the gap between what is actually happening and what we think *should* be happening or are afraid *could* happen. The most important question is: What are you paying attention to? Are you paying attention to your direct experience here and now or to the desires, hopes, dreams, worries, doubts, and fears running through your thoughts?

It is easier to suffer when we are having a very intense experience whether that intensity comes from extreme sensations from illness or injury, or from extreme experiences of loss or limitation, or both. When the experience is extreme, the slightest gap between the experience and what we are paying attention to can cause extreme suffering. In contrast, during more ordinary experiences the gap can be larger before suffering arises. In ordinary moments, your attention can wander a fair amount before any suffering becomes noticeable. It will have to wander a long ways into a mental story about how things could or should be different before the suffering becomes intense.

The key to not suffering even when there is great difficulty, limitation, loss, or pain is to give 100% of your attention to the experience just as it is. If there is pain, then notice everything you can about the sensations in your body in this very moment. Then notice how those sensations have changed or shifted in the very next moment. Anytime you do this, you will find that the suffering quickly dissipates, even if the sensations don't.

If there is an emotional, practical, or financial setback or loss, then notice the actual experience in this moment and the next moment and so on. The more intense or extreme the loss or sensations or emotions, the more critical it is to keep your attention completely in the present moment.

With this approach, our most difficult experiences can become our greatest opportunities to move into a direct way of being that is free of suffering or at least freer of suffering. Suffering is caused by thought and, therefore, the suffering itself is just a thought. The good news is that even when we let our attention wander to a fear, hope or desire and begin to suffer, there is no harm done. In the very next breath we can bring our attention back to the here and now, and the suffering will disappear. Recognizing this can bring a sense of holding all of life lightly as we move in and out of moments of suffering and moments of greater presence and ease. Sometimes the best we can do is have compassion for ourselves and for the often overwhelming circumstances of our life, and then perhaps bring just a little more attention to the experience we are having in this moment just as it is.

It is not at all easy to do this under extreme circumstances, and I am so sorry that life is testing you so drastically. But it is possible to not suffer under any circumstances, and it is really this simple. My teacher, Neelam, used to say that if only life was more complicated, we all would have figured it out a long time ago!

I wrote more about the cause of suffering in this article:

The Gap in Awareness

We usually think that suffering is caused by bad experiences, but it's actually caused by our attention flowing towards something that's not really there, towards something that's not very true in that moment, such as an idea or a fantasy, which are very small truths. Suffering ends when our attention flows towards what's actually happening, what's true in the moment. Suffering is the distance--the gap-- between what you're oriented towards and what is. However large the gap is between what's actually happening and what you're putting your attention on is how much you will suffer. If there's no gap, there's no suffering.

That gap can be present regardless of whether something good or bad is happening. For example, if someone close to you is dying, your awareness may be so fully focused on what's happening in that moment that the experience lacks the suffering you would expect, although suffering may appear later if thoughts creep in about how things should have or could have been. In contrast, there are times when things are going really well and you're suffering, often because you're afraid of things changing. If this truth is understood--that it doesn't matter what happens--it can change your life. This understanding may or may not change what's happening, but it will change your experience of what's happening.

Our hopes, dreams, desires, fears, doubts, and worries aren't really happening, so they are very small truths. When we give our attention to something that isn't actually happening, we suffer. When our attention is focused on these things, we never feel satisfied because they don't nourish us. But when we give our passion and curiosity to more of what's true in the moment, we don't suffer. What are you giving your awareness, your passion, your curiosity to?

It's very simple: Our suffering is a matter of how much of our attention is flowing towards what's not actually present, such as hopes, dreams, desires, fears, doubts, worries, ideals, and fantasies. What we're desiring isn't present (except in our imagination), or we wouldn't be desiring it. Nor is what we fear. Our fears are just as much a figment of our imagination as our desires. None of these things are real, and turning our attention towards the unreal brings us out of contact with the real, where the aliveness of Being can be experienced.

Rejection and desire are the mechanisms with which we resist what is, which results in our suffering. They operate in a cycle: We go back and forth from rejection to desire. We think, "This isn't good. Maybe if I got this or if I meditated more or if only I had a better lover or more money or more freedom, it could be better." Then we go about trying to fulfill that desire and, regardless of whether we succeed or not, we come back to the point where we still reject whatever is present now. Even when we get what we think we want, we may find that it's not that great, so we dream up something else we believe will make things better.

This activity of desiring what isn't present and rejecting what is creates and sustains the sense of a small self. If things are lousy, they're lousy for whom? For me. And if things could be better, better for whom? Better for me. We're often not even conscious of rejecting and desiring because we're caught up in the content of our desires and fantasies. We get so hypnotized by our fantasies that we're not even aware they're contracting our sense of self and making us feel very small, incomplete, deficient, and unsatisfied.

Nevertheless, that sense of incompleteness can be trusted. It's telling you how true it is that your fantasy will make you feel better. The sense of incompleteness and smallness in the experience of fantasizing shows you just how little truth there is in your fantasy. Fantasies aren't very true. They only exist in our minds. There isn't much substance or reality to them.

You can also trust when your heart feels very full and complete. The simple alternative to rejection and desire is to give all your attention to what is here right now. The only trick is to include all of what is present right now. Every sensation can be included. There is no suffering in any sensation that you give all of your attention to. The suffering comes in when we have an idea about the sensation that pulls us away from it.

The biggest surprise is that ultimately there is no suffering even in our suffering! When you give all of your attention to the actual experience of rejection and desire, the suffering inherent in it dissolves. When we become curious and attentive to the process of rejection, it no longer has any sting. If you simply become fully present to the movement of thought, it can be recognized for what it really is: just a thought! Suffering is like a mirage that you never actually reach. It dissolves whenever you get close to it.

Nothing Is Included

Everything is included in the unfolding mystery of life. Every object, action, person, thought, feeling, desire, and more make up the whole fabric of existence. Thoughts, feelings, and desires are more subtle than objects and overt actions, but they still have a kind of reality and, at times, a profound effect on us and the unfolding of life. More subtle aspects of our Being, such as love, peace, joy, wisdom, clarity, and compassion, can have an even more profoundly transformative effect on our experience, even though they are even more subtle than feelings and desires.

There is something else that is still more subtle and hard to grasp, and that is nothing or emptiness. And yet, this most subtle aspect of our existence, the no-thingness of empty space, is also the most powerful and radically transformative part of life. Space is infinite in both dimension and in potential. It is the biggest "thing" or "no-thing" that we can experience. Everywhere you go, there is space. There is so much space that the entire universe is in constant motion, and yet, only rarely do things collide. If you add up all of the motions that our planet, solar system, and galaxy are engaged in, we are traveling right now at over 1,000,000 miles per hour! Thank goodness, there is so much space, so we can zip around that fast and not run into anything!

Because space is so empty and ever-present, we tend to overlook it and take it for granted. We are deeply conditioned to ignore emptiness or even to see it as a problem. We often see it as a lack or deficiency that needs to be filled or fixed. This in part stems from some of our earliest experiences of the physical body: when our stomach is empty as a baby, that emptiness is a problem. That emptiness needs to be filled and preferably now! This results in conditioning that perceives emptiness as something that needs to be filled.

Later in life, when we encounter a more subtle experience of emptiness, such as an experience of not knowing or nothing much happening or someone not paying attention to us, we tend to interpret those experience as another lack that needs to be filled—and preferably now! So we become very busy trying to fill these subtler empty sensations with external objects or stimulation. This can translate into eating more food or pursuing other experiences to excess, such as sex, romance, shopping, drugs or alcohol, surfing the web. Almost any activity or object can be pursued in an addictive manner when we are using them to try to fill an inner sense of emptiness.

There is another possibility: we can stop and simply experience and explore the space, nothingness, emptiness, or lack that is present right now. What is the space or sense of lack like in this moment? Where is it located in your body? What is it like to not know something? What is it like to just sit and be still when nothing is happening? Is emptiness or the absence of something actually a bad sensation, or just a particular sensation? If you stop trying to fill it for a moment, is it still uncomfortable or is it just quiet, still, and empty?

Emptiness or space is the softest thing in the universe. No thing or nothing is the one thing that cannot hurt you. There is an absence of an elephant sitting in your lap right now. Is the absence of an elephant uncomfortable or painful?

If not, then is the absence of excitement, pleasure, knowing, love, or happiness actually uncomfortable? Or is that absence just empty, light, and spacious like the absence of the elephant?

When we can just be with silence, stillness, and nothingness, we discover something truly startling: space or emptiness is the source of everything. Space is not just limitless in dimension, it also contains limitless energy and potential. Everything that exists comes out of pure, formless space. Emptiness is the Source of all existence and all phenomena, from the most subtle to the most physical and dense. Emptiness is the source of everything that really matters in life: peace, joy, love, clarity, wisdom, insight, compassion, pleasure, satisfaction, value, integrity, and awareness itself.

The more we simply rest and are with a sensation of lack or something missing, the more we experience the subtle flow of emptiness into form. Surprisingly, when we allow the feelings of lack, emptiness, absence, dryness, boredom, unworthiness, unlovable-ness, and unsafe-ness to simply be here, the thing that seemed to be missing often is what shows up. In the space where love seems to be the most absent, is where true love most often arises.

What a shock! Everything we could ever want or need is already here as pure potential in the very place where it seemed to be missing. This turns the whole world inside out. Emptiness is the source, not the problem! There is a natural flow from emptiness into form, and it is at this empty source that we are filled and satisfied in life.

In contrast, the world of form and objects is actually a movement of form back into emptiness. When we focus exclusively on the objects, sensations, and experiences that are already present, we discover that nothing lasts. Everything that exists is changing and dissolving back into formless energy and then space, potentially leaving us feeling bereft. There is nothing wrong with everything that exists. It is all part of the miracle of life and Being. Everything is included. However, every "thing" is a temporary, passing phenomenon. Attaching to any "thing" will lead to a feeling of loss or disappointment.

Nothing, emptiness, space is the one reality that is eternal and unchanging. But nothing is not really no "thing." Nothing is the infinite potential of Being at total rest. When nothing is happening, there is limitless potential for anything to happen. Empty space is like a flashlight that is turned off. The light is still there, but it is there in potential instead of in form or action. When you flick the switch, then that potential light or energy is released into action. The formless nature of empty space is like having the switch of all possibility and every expression turned off. With even the subtlest movement of consciousness, the light of existence shines forth into form.

Everything is included, from the most gross to the most subtle, from physical objects to energy, to love and joy, to the most subtle expression of potential we call awareness or consciousness. All of these are expressions of the limitless potential of Being. The most subtle dimension is no expression, or pure emptiness. Whatever you imagine emptiness or nothingness to be, you can still subtract that image to get a more direct sense of how purely empty of all form the Absolute or Source is.

Why not be curious about all of the dimensions of existence that are here, including the pure emptiness of infinite space? If everything is included, then nothing has to be included too.

Appendix 1: The Heart's Wisdom

The following is from Living from the Heart *by Nirmala, which is available for free at http://endless-satsang.com/free*

The Heart's Wisdom

The truth is that which opens the heart. The capacity to sense the truth is something we all already have. We all have a heart that is already accurately showing us how true things are.

Anything that puts you in touch with more of the truth opens the heart. This is a literal and experiential description of truth. When your experience is bringing you more truth, there is a sense of opening, softening, relaxation, expansion, fulfillment, and satisfaction in the heart. This can be most directly sensed in the center of the chest, but the heart of all Being is infinite and therefore actually bigger than your entire body. So this opening, softening, and expansion is actually happening everywhere; we just sense it most clearly and directly in the center of the chest.

When you encounter truth, the sense of your self opens, expands, softens, fills in, and lets go. The me, the sense of your self, is no longer felt to be so limited or small. It becomes more complete and unbounded. The boundaries soften and dissolve, and any sense of inadequacy, limitation, or deficiency is lessened or eliminated.

As a side effect of being in touch with more of the truth, your mind gets quieter because you simply have less to think about. Even knowing a simple truth like where your car keys are gives you less to think about. And when you touch upon a very large truth, your mind becomes even quieter, like when you see the ocean for the first time: The truth or reality you're viewing is so immense that, at least for a moment, your mind is stopped and becomes very quiet.

In contrast, when your experience is moving into a diminished or smaller experience of the truth and of reality, the heart contracts. The sense of your self gets tight, hard, contracted, and feels incomplete, bounded, and limited. It can feel like you are small, inadequate, or unworthy. The smallness of the truth is reflected in the smallness of the sense of your self. The result of being less in touch with the truth is that your mind gets busier as it tries to figure out what is true.

Fortunately, your Being is never diminished or contracted, only the sense of your self. Just as blocking your view of the whole room by partially covering your eyes makes your sense of the room smaller without actually making the room smaller, an idea or belief that is not very true is reflected in a small sense of your self, without actually limiting or contracting your Being.

This opening and closing of the heart in response to the degree of truth you are experiencing isn't something you need to practice or perfect. Your heart has been accurately and perfectly showing you how true your experience has been all along. If you start to notice your heart's openings and closings, you'll discover that you already have everything you need to determine what is true. The heart is the true inner teacher, the source of inner guidance we all have as our birthright. You don't need a spiritual teacher or spiritual books to show you what is true, just your own heart.

Exercise: Take a moment to sense your heart. Dropping into the heart can help you get more in touch with what is happening there. Notice if the heart feels relatively contracted or relatively open. In either case, your heart is working perfectly to show you the degree of truth you are experiencing in this moment. Also notice if your heart is expanding or contracting in this moment. The movement might be subtle or a fairly gross contraction or relaxation. You may be able to notice that the heart is always shifting in response to every thought, feeling, desire, and experience that arises in your awareness. There is no wrong way for your heart to respond. It is always showing you the relative truth of this moment.

What Is the Truth?

Truth is what exists, what is here now. So if what exists is also what is true, then there is only truth. Whatever is present is true—but to varying degrees. Just as there is no actual substance or energy that is darkness, but just varying amounts of the energy of light or photons, there is no falsehood or untruth, only varying degrees of the truth.

We are always experiencing the truth. But because we don't experience everything in any one moment, our experience of truth is always limited. Sometimes we experience a large amount of truth—of what is actually here—and sometimes we experience only a small amount of what is actually happening, of what is true. Our heart's openness or lack of openness in each moment is what shows us how much of the truth is being experienced in any moment.

What about ideas that are mistaken? An idea or belief that has little or no correspondence to external reality is going to be an extremely small truth, so small it may only exist in one person's mind, like the saying: "He was a legend in his own mind." When you experience an erroneous idea or belief, your heart will contract appropriately to show you that it is a very small and inconsequential truth.

For example, if you entertain the idea that you will never be happy unless you have ten million dollars, your heart will contract appropriately to show you that it is just an idea. This contraction may be very quick, so quick that it doesn't cause you any discomfort or trouble. But if you really believe this, then the sense of your self will contract for as long as that idea is held.

Exercise: For just a moment, hold onto a limiting thought, such as "I will never have enough time," and notice the response in your heart. Does that thought allow you to relax and be, or does it require a kind of effort or contraction just to hold it? Now consider another thought that you find ridiculous because it is so untrue, such as "I will never be happy unless I become President of the United States." Notice how it might not even be possible to hold onto this thought. It might even make you laugh. Many jokes end with a ridiculously impossible truth (e.g., "And then the dog said to its owner, 'I guess I should have said Dimaggio instead of Ruth') and the smallness of the truth of the punch line causes you to let go of believing in it. Laughter is a wonderful movement into a bigger perspective!

Thoughts are real—they exist—but they still exist only as ideas. You could put all the thoughts ever thought into a pile, and they still wouldn't trip anybody. They only exist as neural firings in the brain, so to focus on thoughts exclusively is to severely limit or contract your experience of reality and therefore the sense of your self.

In the range of everyday experience, our ideas have varying degrees of correspondence with reality. Those that correspond more closely to reality won't contract or limit the sense of self for as long as mistaken ones. Many ideas are of service to our ability to be at ease in the world. For example, when you need to go someplace, correct ideas about how to get there allow you to simply go there and then move on to other experiences. Ideas such as these can enhance our experience, rather than limit or contract it. An idea about where something is located is, of course, not a big truth, but it's also not usually experienced as a limiting one.

The Heart's Capacity to Show You the Truth

All there is, is truth, and our heart's capacity to reflect the degree of truth in any experience is the way we recognize how true a particular experience is.

What is this heart? What is this sense of self that is ever present? It doesn't relate to sensations in the physical heart or chest. It's a more subtle sense, at times even more subtle than the physical senses, although the opening or contracting can also be experienced as relaxation and contraction in the physical body. The sense of your self, the sense that you exist, is something more intimate than your physical experience.

What does it mean when you say me? What are you referring to when you say me? This simple fact that we are here, that we exist, is a very mysterious aspect of our experience. When we speak of it poetically to try to capture its essence, we call it the heart, like when you know something in your heart or when your heart is touched.

This sense of your self is a very alive and changing experience. At times, your sense of me is open, free-flowing, and expanded. At other times, like when a judgment arises, it feels small, inadequate, and deficient. In these moments, have you actually changed? Has your body suddenly shrunk? Much of the time this sense of me is bigger than or smaller than your physical body. How does that work? Have you ever experienced your inner child? How can your me be the size of a child when you are an adult?

The sense of me, the sense of self, is shifting all the time. It's always either opening and expanding, or contracting and tightening, similar to the ongoing expansion and contraction of our breathing.

Exercise: Consider the idea that it is better to be thinner or more beautiful or younger than you are, and notice what happens to the sense of your self. Does your heart open, soften, and expand? Does this idea allow you to simply be? Or does it tighten and restrict the flow of your experience?

Then just for contrast, notice what happens to the sense of your self if you consider the idea that you are okay just the way you are. It might be challenging to consider this idea without other thoughts being triggered, such as "But I'm not really good enough!" If this happens, your heart will show you how true this response is, not how true the original idea of okayness is.

Just as an experiment, see if you can hold the idea that you're okay just the way you are, and then notice what happens in your heart. Does this idea allow your heart to open, soften, and expand? Does it allow you to simply be? Or does it tighten and restrict the flow of your experience? For most, the idea of being okay just the way they are allows a greater ease and fullness to the experience of the self.

The idea that it is better to be thinner, more beautiful, or younger than you are is simply a smaller truth than the idea that you are perfect the way you are. Even if you are beautiful, thin, or young, the idea that it is better to be that way can limit the sense of your self. If it's better to be that way, can you just relax and be, or do you need to do something to stay that way?

In contrast, a neutral idea that doesn't state or imply anything about you can be experienced neutrally in your sense of self. For example, if you consider the color of the ceiling in someone else's house, this usually won't open or close your heart because it's not about you and probably doesn't imply anything about you. The sense of your self doesn't shift in response to neutral ideas like this.

This opening and closing of the heart is not a prescription—something you need to practice—but simply a description of what your heart has been doing your entire life. Whatever does happen in the sense of self in any moment is entirely correct and appropriate. It's appropriate for your heart to close when someone is telling you a small, limiting truth; and it's appropriate for your heart to open when you experience a deep and profound reality.

The Heart's Quickness

Your heart is incredibly quick. It instantly knows how true something is and instantly opens or closes to that degree. It's so fast that it never really lands anywhere. It is always either opening or closing in response to each moment.

So if a thought triggers another thought, the heart will then be reflecting the relative truth of the triggered thought, not the original one. And if this triggered thought triggers another one, then your heart will reflect how true the latest thought is. The openness of your heart can shift very rapidly, as rapidly as you can think another thought!

I was working with a woman once who had difficulty taking time for herself. I asked her to check in her heart to see how true it is that it is okay to take time for herself. She closed her eyes for a moment, and when I asked her what had happened, she said she felt an intense contraction. I was surprised, so I asked her to tell me exactly what had happened. She said she thought, "It's okay to take time for myself," and then immediately decided this would be selfish, and her heart contracted. Her heart was showing her how true it was that it would be selfish to take time for herself. It was no longer reflecting the truth of the idea that it is okay to take time for herself.

In the quickness of our usual rapid-fire thinking, it can be tricky to determine what your heart is actually responding to. Therefore, when checking in your heart to see how true something is, it is helpful to slow down and take each thought or each possibility one at a time.

Exercise: Take a moment to think about a situation in your life. Notice if there are any familiar or recurring thoughts about that situation. Pick one of the main ideas, beliefs, opinions, or attitudes you have about that situation or about someone or something related to it. Now just hold that thought gently in your awareness. Repeat it to yourself a few times, and as you do, notice what happens in your heart. Does it open and soften, or is there a kind of tightness or hardness that starts to form in your awareness? Remember, either way your heart is working perfectly to show you how true the thought is.

See if you can hold that one simple thought for a moment, almost like a child completely engrossed in whatever he or she is looking at. Holding a thought for a moment gives you a clearer picture of the relative truth of that thought, as indicated by your heart's response while you are focusing completely on it.

If your mind wanders and you find yourself having second and third thoughts, or even a whole conversation with yourself about the situation, that's fine. Just note that the heart has moved on along with your thoughts and is now showing you the truth of the thought you are having in this moment.

The Role of Judgments

Not only can an initial thought or experience trigger other thoughts, the opening or closing of your heart can itself trigger a thought or judgment that results in the further closing of the heart and a sense of your self as limited or small. If you are a spiritual seeker and have come to believe that it is better for your heart to be open than closed, then a sudden contraction of the sense of your self can trigger a further judgment related to not wanting to be contracted, which closes the heart even further. Test it for yourself:

Exercise: If you hold the idea that you shouldn't feel contracted, does your heart open? Does that idea allow you to just be? Or does it tighten or limit the sense of your self? The idea that you shouldn't feel contracted is a limiting idea and usually feels tight or limited because it is simply not very true.

There is a certain kind of logic to this cycle of judgment, even though it results in a restricted sense of self: When the sense of your self contracts, your awareness also contracts and becomes limited, and your unawareness expands. When your field of awareness becomes smaller, the rest of reality lies outside your awareness in that moment. The logic of judgment is based on this simple effect. As a result of a judgment, you become less aware of your experience and temporarily less aware of the initial discomfort that triggered the judgment. Therefore, you get some relief from it. The logic of judgment is based on this temporary relief provided by the reduction in your awareness.

However, the flaw in this logic is that now that contraction of your awareness must be maintained or you will become aware again of the initial discomfort. Maintaining a contraction is, itself, uncomfortable. Try making a tight fist and holding it for several moments. It will quickly begin to feel uncomfortable. Similarly, when you keep your awareness contracted to avoid an uncomfortable sensation, this generates even more discomfort.

So when a cycle of judgment is triggered, the sense of your self and your awareness keep getting smaller as you try to avoid the ever-increasing discomfort caused by this same contraction of your sense of self and your awareness. This often continues until you are exhausted by the effort involved in maintaining vigilance against your discomfort, and you simply let go of any judgment.

The good news is that whenever you are not contracting your sense of self through small truths, such as judgments, the sense of your self naturally relaxes and opens. An open, spacious sense of self is the natural resting state of your Being, just as your muscles naturally lengthen and expand in the absence of any effort to contract them. So when a cycle of judgment wears you out, there is sometimes a profound release of the small sense of self and the contraction of awareness. In light of this, it's not surprising that many realizations and spiritual awakenings occur immediately following an extremely contracted and painful experience.

More good news is that the tendency to judge is not your fault. You were taught to do it by those who raised you, who were taught by those who raised them. They did this because it was the best way they knew to manage their own discomfort. When parents are confronted with the unlimited Being of a two year-old (and we all know how big that can be), they often resort to the best means they know for giving that two year-old a more limited sense of his or her Being: judgment.

We eventually learned to do this for ourselves. We learned to judge ourselves and hold limiting ideas about ourselves to get along with the people around us, especially those who clothed and fed us.

Judgment is just one of the many ways we limit our experience of the truth and thereby limit our experience of our self. Other culprits are our ideas, beliefs, opinions, concepts, doubts, fears, worries, hopes, dreams, desires, and our usual knowledge. Judgment is just one of the more effective ways of limiting the sense of our self because it always implies something limiting about the self.

Exercise: Make a list of some of the judgments you have about yourself, life, and other people. Pick ones that you really believe. Now read through your list several times and notice the sense you have of yourself as you do this. Does holding these judgments give you a sense of yourself as someone in particular, someone who has a very definite perspective on life? Do you feel more connected with others and with the world, or do you feel more separate and apart from the world? Even if that separate sense of self feels superior because it has the right judgments, how big or open and relaxed is your sense of self when you have these judgments?

This implied someone in all of your judgments is always a small someone, someone who is limited and therefore vulnerable to something bad or who needs to feel superior or for something good to happen to feel better or even survive. The ultimate truth is that you are unlimited. Your Being can never be harmed—or benefited—by any experience. Only a smaller (less true) idea of your self can seem to be harmed or benefited.

Positive Judgment

What was said about negative judgments applies to positive judgments as well. When some experience triggers a positive judgment, the sense of our self contracts just as much as when we have a negative judgment. Test this for yourself:

Exercise: Think about something you have a very strong positive judgment of, like your favorite movie or something you have done that you are very proud of. Notice what happens to the sense of your self when you have a positive thought about this. If you find yourself thinking something like, "Great! This is wonderful—wait until I tell my friends!" notice what happens to the sense of your self. You may be surprised to find that your heart isn't as open as it was before the positive judgment. A big truth allows you to relax and just be however you are and to change in any way that naturally happens. A positive idea about your self implies that you have to continue to be a certain way to be okay.

Implied even in positive judgments is an idea of yourself as someone who is limited—someone who needs good things to happen to be okay and feel adequate. There's nothing wrong with something good happening; it's just that even your positive judgments are small truths that are based on a small idea of your self. Your heart will contract just as much for a small positive truth as for a small negative truth.

Fortunately, there's nothing you need to do about a small truth beyond recognizing it's small. Besides, even small truths can be useful. So there is no need to try to rid yourself of them, which isn't even possible. Seeing that they are small immediately puts them in perspective. Then, when they arise, they are seen as no big deal. You might still think them, but no matter how often they arise, you recognize them as relatively unimportant.

You have probably experienced this ability of a bigger truth to displace or put in perspective a smaller truth. For example, if you or someone you love is suddenly diagnosed with a life-threatening disease, what really matters becomes obvious. The truth, or reality, of a possible death makes many other truths appear small and insignificant in comparison.

You don't need to wait for a big truth to hit you over the head to put your experience in perspective. Simply notice how true each thought is. Experiences come in all different sizes. You are always moving in and out of different degrees of truth, and you are naturally able to discriminate how true each one is. You can determine how truly important something is just by noticing the content of your thought and the sense of self it results in. If it opens and relaxes the sense of your self, your heart, then it is truly important. If it contracts or limits the sense of your self, your heart, then it's not.

All Truth Is Relative

Truth is all there is. Yet our experience of truth, of reality, is always partial. Right now your field of vision is partial. You can only see what is in front of you, not what's behind you. Similarly, your heart is always showing you the degree of truth of the experience you are having in the moment.

Your view or range of experience is always opening and closing, filling in the blanks in your experience or forgetting or ignoring parts of your experience. Whenever you focus on a particular aspect of experience, you necessarily stop noticing other aspects. As a result, any particular perspective is either smaller and more limited, larger and more complete, or roughly the same degree of completeness as another perspective.

The openness of the sense of your self is always relative. Because truth is always relative, any particular truth could be experienced as an opening or a closing of your heart. Even a small experience of the truth may be larger than the experience you were just having and therefore will be experienced as an opening or relaxation in your heart. Similarly, even a fairly large truth can feel limiting if you move into it from an even larger, more spacious experience.

For example, if you've lived most of your life paying attention to your thoughts and ideas, then the first time you are put in touch with your emotions will be experienced as an expansion of consciousness. It will feel like you've discovered a new, rich dimension of your Being.

However, if you've had many even larger experiences of much more expanded states of Being, possibly through spiritual practices, then moving into a strong emotion like anger, sadness, or excitement may be experienced as a contraction or diminishment of the sense of your self. The same truth, the same experience of emotion, can be experienced as either an opening up in your heart or a closing down. It just depends on where you move into the emotion from and also how open or expanded the sense of your self generally is.

The difference can be slight between two experiences with similar degrees of truth or unimaginably huge. The true dimensions of your Being are limitless. You are everything, and when you directly experience this completeness, the sense of self can be equally vast and limitless.

Your Perfect Wisdom

Your heart is the wisest thing in the universe. The sense of your self is always perfectly and accurately showing you how true things are, how complete your perspective is in every moment. Even when your heart is contracted because of some deeply conditioned idea you are holding, it is appropriately and accurately wise in its contraction.

No one has more capacity to distinguish how true things are than anyone else. No one is wiser than you, and no one is less wise than you. Since no one else is able to experience your individual perspective, no one else can ever be more of an expert on your experience than you. Just as someone else can't eat and digest your breakfast for you, others can't experience and digest your perspective of the truth in each moment.

If no heart is any wiser than any other, perhaps that's because there is just one heart that functions through many bodies and yet is not contained in any of these particular expressions. What you are is this one heart of Being.

Since we are all equally endowed with the wisdom of the heart, there is no need to give away our authority to another. There is nothing better than your own heart at discriminating how true something is for you right now.

In addition, the thoughts that cause contraction are not your fault. Your thoughts and beliefs were passed on to you by others, who learned them from others. If you trace each conditioned thought or reaction back to its source, you'll discover that all limiting beliefs and ideas are shared among us all. If anyone is to blame for them, it's all of us put together. Another way you could say this is that the whole of Being is the source of everything, even the limited ways we have of experiencing that Being.

With this understanding, the possibility exists to simply trust your heart, no matter how big or small the truth is that you are experiencing. You can trust your heart when it opens, and you can trust it when it closes. Your heart is the wisest and most trustworthy thing there is. In the deepest spiritual traditions, the true teacher, or satguru, is seen to be within each of us. Your true teacher is this sensitive and accurate heart, which expands and contracts as it senses the endless folding and unfolding of life.

Applying Your Heart's Wisdom

Because the heart responds so quickly to what's happening now. . . and now. . . and now, it's helpful to slow down and take your experience one thought or response at a time if you wish to find out how true it is. Just as you can more fully appreciate a meal if you take each bite and savor it, the possibility exists to take time to fully sense a thought that arises.

For example, let's say you remember a disappointing experience and then the thought arises, "My life will never be good enough." Before you rush into thinking of all the ways this is true or, alternatively, defending yourself with reasons why it isn't true, you might take a moment to sense directly how this thought affects the sense of your self. Then, when you know for yourself how true this thought is all by itself, it may be obvious that it is neither completely true nor completely false. If it is sensed directly as a relatively small truth about your life, it may not even be necessary to defend against it with an opposing thought. Sensing how true an initial thought is in this way can reduce the importance of any ensuing thoughts.

Another practical way of exploring and utilizing your heart's truth-sensing capacity is to check in your heart when making a choice. By doing that, you can find out what choice is the truer one. However, when it comes to relative choices (e.g., what to do, what to eat, where to live, who to marry, etc.), the differences may be slight in your heart. From the ultimate perspective, the practical choices we make in life may not be that important. So it may take a while to learn to accurately sense the differences in how true various choices are. But just as a wine connoisseur can learn to discriminate the subtlest difference in flavors, you can learn to sense even very small differences in how true a choice is relative to another.

When checking in your heart for the truth about some choice, it's helpful to consider as many choices as possible. The truest one may be somewhere in between the possibilities you've considered, or it may be something completely different. For example, a friend was torn between her desire to go permanently on spiritual retreat and her desire to stay with her husband. Neither option felt completely true in her heart. When I suggested that maybe she could stay with her husband but still go away for long periods of time on spiritual retreats, her heart opened, as she sensed this was the truest way to respond to both desires.

Exercise: Think of a choice you are considering in your life. It might be best to pick something where you have a decision to make that isn't too important and not too immediate so that you can really explore the process of comparing the truth of your choices. Make a list of possible choices you could make, and be sure to include some that are in between or completely different from the first two options you come up with.

Now really take some time with each choice and sense your heart's response as you hold in mind the idea of making that choice. Again, keep it simple, and just picture having made the choice, and let go of secondary considerations, such as pros and cons and further ramifications. Notice whether considering a particular choice results in a spacious, easeful sense in your heart or a contracted sense of your own self. There is no right or wrong way for your heart to respond. Just notice the way it does respond.

Include the thought that it doesn't matter what you choose. In many cases, the biggest truth about your choices is that what you choose doesn't really matter. If that is the case, then that thought or perspective will give you the most room to just be, and the largest sense of yourself.

Finally, when considering the relative truth of various possible choices, it is also helpful to check in your heart several times over a period of time. Especially when making major life choices, checking numerous times before acting is more likely to result in a more satisfying outcome. For example, if you want to know if it's true to stay in an intimate relationship, you might find a different result right after an argument than right after your lover has surprised you with a gift. It's a bigger perspective to find out what is truest over the long term than just what is true in the present moment.

The heart is wise and accurate and can show you how true it is to stay or go, how true it is to buy a house, how true it is to take a new job, even how true it is to eat another cookie. But it also can show you much more of the possibilities inherent in this life and much more of the truth of your Being. In relation to these bigger truths, the practical questions of your life turn out to be relatively small matters. Using your heart only to know things like what to do or where to live is like using a global positioning satellite system to find your way from your bedroom to your bathroom. It utilizes only a small part of your heart's capacity.

However, following your heart day in and day out can put you in touch with the richness of the functioning of this dimension of your Being. Along the way, you may also find your heart opening in response to the bigger truths and deeper movements of Being that touch every life.

Exercise: For a moment, sense if there is any Peace here. Don't worry how much or if there's only a little bit of Peace here right now. Just notice if you can sense any Peace at all. Now focus your attention on that Peace that is here beneath the flow of thoughts or feelings. Give yourself permission to really sense the nature of Peace and the deep stillness in that experience. As you touch Peace with your awareness, notice if there really is any boundary to the stillness at the core of this moment. Don't worry about doing this right, but just taste as much of the Peace that is here right now as you can.

Now notice the sense of your own Being. Focusing on Peace may have relaxed or opened your sense of self profoundly or just a little. Notice if this has softened or expanded your heart.

The Many Sizes of Truth

The deepest and largest truths don't fit into words or language. While words can act as pointers, your heart will open the widest and the sense of your self will feel the most complete and full in response to the direct experience of the vast dimensions of Being that are beyond thoughts and beliefs. As always, your own heart is the truest guide to these larger dimensions and possibilities, but the reason the sense of your self expands when your view of the truth is more complete is because you are the truth. You are everything that exists. When you are experiencing more of the truth, you are experiencing more of your self.

The truth comes in many different sizes. One of the primary ways you create and maintain a small sense of self is through a profound involvement with thought. We've been taught from an early age to think, conceptualize, and name things. Because there is such a huge momentum to thinking, moments without a thought happening are rare. Thinking is such a prevalent part of our moment-to-moment experience that many of us live mostly in our minds.

Adding to this momentum of thought are strongly held assumptions and beliefs about the world and yourself, many of which are unconscious. This deeper current of thought also serves to create and maintain a small, separate sense of self. As a result of all of our conscious thinking and unconscious assumptions and beliefs, most people live in awareness of a very small part of reality, most of which only exists in their mind.

This momentum of small truths is reflected in a momentum to your small sense of self. This leads to the question of what to do about it. Unfortunately, any idea about what to do about it is just that—an idea, another thought. However, what is possible is to simply be aware of the prevalence of thought in your experience. This awareness is not really something you do, as awareness is a fundamental quality of what you are. Just as you don't need to do anything to have shoulders, you don't need to do anything extra right now to be aware—and to be aware of your thinking.

Exercise: What is thinking like right now? You can notice not only the content of your thoughts, but also the rhythm and speed of your thoughts, the ebb and flow of thought. Where do thoughts come from and where do they go? What happens if there is a pause between thoughts?

How is the sense of your self affected by this flow of thought? Do you need to think in order to be? Does thinking give your sense of self a familiar smallness and sense of boundaries? Is it uncomfortable to not know something in this moment, to not have a thought?

The invitation is to just notice thought and its effect on the sense of your self. Any idea of changing your experience is just another thought that will have a similar effect on the sense of your self. Why not simply find out what thought is like? Experience for yourself how true each thought is. There's nothing wrong with small truths – they're just small. What if all of your thinking is not that big a deal? What if your thinking is just not a very large container for the truth? Thinking can only contain a small amount of the truth.

There is no need to get rid of thought. Once you experience that thought is not a very large container for the truth, this gives way to another question: What else is here besides thought? What else is true? As you sense the prevalence of thought and possibly even the deeper current of unconscious beliefs and assumptions, you may also begin to sense what surrounds and contains thought.

Drop into your heart and notice the space all around your thoughts. What effect does dropping into your heart have on your sense of self?

The Deeper Currents of Thought

Many beliefs and assumptions shape and limit our experience of truth and the sense of our self even when we aren't consciously thinking them. They are ideas and concepts that are so deeply believed that they aren't even questioned, such as "Life is short" or "There's never enough time." Furthermore, these beliefs and assumptions generate other thoughts, which add to the momentum of thinking and keep your heart, the sense of your self, small and contracted.

Two deeper currents of thought strongly shape the experience of your self. The first is the belief in a direction to your life. Usually this direction is toward more, different, or better experiences. But sometimes it's framed in opposite terms as not less, the same, or not worse. In either case, there is a deeply held belief that life should move or change in a particular way.

Of course, things do change, which keeps the hope alive that they will change in the way you want them to. This deeply held assumption that things could or should be better implies a small you. The directionality of this assumption is based on a reference point: Things should be better — for you. If things should be better for you, then you must be lacking something. This assumption and the thinking it generates help maintain a small, contracted sense of your self because that is the implied reference point of the assumption — a small you.

The second, even deeper and less conscious current of thought that serves to maintain a contracted sense of self is the assumption that physical experience is the most real. This is such a widely held assumption that any other orientation could get you labeled crazy. Even very sensitive and spiritually-oriented people who have had very real and profound experiences of other dimensions are often pulled by this assumption back toward the physical into a more limited experience of truth and their own Being.

There are many dimensions to reality besides the purely physical, and as a human being, your experience includes all of these dimensions. There are the dimensions of thought, emotion, and intuition. And beyond those, are dimensions of pure presence and spacious Being. Many of these dimensions are more real than even physical reality. Experiences of this transcendent reality give you a transcendent sense of your self that is much fuller and more complete than the purely physical sense of your self.

The Thought That You Are the Body

The idea that your life could or should be better and the idea that physical reality is the most real animate an even more basic assumption: that you are the body. Your sense of your self, and therefore the experience of your Being, is most often shaped and limited by your identification with the body, which results in the ongoing question, How is it going for the body? Is it better, more pleasurable, or at least not painful right now for the body? This orientation toward the body isn't bad, but it is a limited way of experiencing reality and your self. It's like watching only one channel on your television: It's something, but it's limited.

This limitation can affect every experience you have. By focusing on how it's going for your body, you can miss some of the richest and most profound possibilities in life. The biggest truths may not even be particularly comfortable for your body. Profound states of love and bliss can be exhausting from a purely physical perspective. The deepest realizations of the nature of your Being can be so vast and expansive as to feel like a death for your identity as the body.

Asking what you can do about this limitation will only reinforce it. Another possibility is to explore the sense of limitation that identification with the body gives to your awareness and your heart.

Exercise: What is it like to believe you are the body right now? Does this allow your heart to open and relax? Or does it result in a small sense of your self? There is nothing wrong with small truths; they just aren't very complete. You don't have to get rid of or change small truths. Just recognizing they are small is enough.

With the recognition of the incompleteness of identifying with the body, a larger curiosity often arises: What else is true about you? Are you more than the body? What other channels are there on this television called your life? What else is going on here?

The Sense of Me

Beneath the assumption that you are the body is an even deeper one. The idea that you are the body is predicated on the assumption that you exist, that you are a me—a separate, individual self. The most intimate sense of your self is often this sense of me, which is a limited and incomplete sensing of your self. It doesn't include the far reaches of your greater Being. This sense of a separate me is not bad or wrong; it's just limited and incomplete.

In the midst of a very profound and large experience of truth, the sense of your self can become so large and inclusive that it no longer has much of a sense of being your Being. When you awaken to the oneness of all things, the sense of a me can thin out quite dramatically. If you are the couch you are sitting on, the clouds in the sky, and everything else, then it simply doesn't make sense to call it all me. If it is so much more than what you usually take yourself to be, then the term me is just too small.

In a profound experience of truth, the sense of me softens and expands to such a degree that there is only a slight sense of me as a separate self remaining, perhaps just as the observer of the vastness of truth. Beyond these profound experiences of the truth, is the truth itself. When you are in touch with the ultimate truth and the most complete sense of Being, there is nothing separate remaining to sense itself — there is no experience and no experiencer, no heart, and no sense of self. There is only Being.

The experience of bigger truths and even the biggest truth doesn't obliterate your capacity to experience a small truth and therefore a separate self. But with many experiences of shifting in and out of a small sense of self, this separate self feels more like a suit of clothes you can take on and off than like something permanent. As you move in and out of many dimensions of Being and even beyond experience itself, the boundaries between all of these dimensions become very permeable and inconsequential. It turns out that these boundaries are just thoughts anyway. They don't actually separate anything.

The question isn't how to get rid of a small sense of self, but what is the sense of your self like? Is it fixed or is it constantly shifting — opening and closing, expanding and contracting, tightening and loosening, and sometimes even disappearing altogether? The sense of a separate self can therefore be loosely held even though it continues to contract appropriately when a small truth is triggered.

What is your sense of self like right now? What is true right now? Your heart is the only guide you need for exploring even the biggest truths.

There Is Only Love

Anything you or anyone else has ever done has been the movement of love. What shapes the movement of love is the sense of me. What we are always doing is taking care of the self, whether it is a small sense of self or a more expanded one. Whenever that sense of self is contracted and small, we take care of that me. And when it's expanded, we take care of that larger sense of self. All we have ever done is tried to take care of the self in the best way we know how, which is always a loving act.

But, of course, when our actions only take care of a contracted me, they don't take care of or take into account other things. For example, we might take care of our taste buds by eating tasty foods, while ignoring our body's need for nutrition. Or if we are so identified with a feeling that all we can do is take care of it, we may not be taking care of our whole Being. Taking care of only the taste buds or only the emotions is still a loving act, but because it is such a narrow way of loving ourselves, it can be neglectful or even harmful to other aspects of our Being or to others.

If we see love in everything we may be afraid that we will allow rape, murder, and other horribly narrow ways of taking care of a small separate sense of me to continue. Yet in discovering that there is only love, the surprising thing is that our actions naturally become more loving. If we see murder as an evil that needs to be abolished without also seeing its basic loving nature, that is when it makes sense to murder. If murder is really bad, then it makes sense to kill someone who has murdered someone else. Or it even makes sense to kill someone before they kill us. It makes sense to bomb a country before it attacks us. But when we see the loving nature even of murder, we can respond to it in a way that doesn't perpetuate it, even as we work to prevent it.

It is possible to recognize the love that is already inside of us and already acting through all of us. It is in recognizing that love that the possibility exists for even greater recognition of love. Contrarily, when we reject any aspect of love — which includes anything that's happening — the more contracted our experience will be and the less completely loving our actions will be. So in condemning, we actually become more like what we condemn. Seeing the beauty, perfection, and love within something is what allows it to transform, to move into a more complete way of loving.

When the sense of our self expands, our actions aren't really any more loving; they're just more loving toward a more complete view of the self. When our loving actions take care of a larger sense of ourselves, we appear more saint-like because they are taking into account everybody, since we recognize that we are everybody. These actions are still self-gratifying, but they are gratifying to a much broader sense of self.

When the awareness of self becomes even more complete, you come to see that there is ultimately nothing that needs to be changed or fixed. Everything is already fine. The world already is full of love. Your actions and everyone else's are already loving. Whatever Being is doing is Being taking care of itself. That is all it ever does or ever has done.

This leads to an appreciation of everything you do and everything that happens, an appreciation of the way Being moves every time it moves. Love is pouring out everywhere. There's no evidence of the lack of love. What a surprise to discover this in a world that seems so full of problems and things that need to be changed.

True Freedom

In this culture where more is felt to be better, there is often an implication that bigger truths are better. If your heart can open and expand, then it may seem best to find a way to open the darn thing all the way and keep it that way.

However, if you check in your heart right now as you hold the idea that it's better to open your heart and keep it that way, you may be surprised to find that this idea actually feels tight or limiting. It's simply not the biggest truth or the most freeing possibility. An even bigger, freer possibility is to allow the sense of your self to be whatever size it is. If your heart is always accurately and appropriately opening or contracting to show you how true each moment's perspective is, then the best result of experiencing a small truth is for your heart to contract and show you how small that truth is. It can be as liberating to find out that a small truth is small as to find out that a vast dimension of Being is profoundly real. In both cases, the nature of truth has been more fully illuminated.

Once you realize you can trust your heart just the way it is right now, whether it is open or closed, you can just rest within the folding and unfolding of all perspectives. You don't do anything to get rid of the small perspectives, which just arise out of the conditioned parts of your Being, and you don't do anything to bring on the bigger perspectives, which just arise out of the unconditioned parts of your Being. You just rest in the moment as it is.

There is never a need to have a bigger or smaller experience, as Being is still Being even in the small experiences. Its nature is the same, and part of its nature is this capacity to discriminate how true—how complete—a particular perspective is. The small experiences of Being are still an expression of Being's ultimate nature, just as a single drop of water is still wet.

Spiritual seekers often think of liberation as staying in an expanded experience of truth. While expanded experiences are freeing (especially when you've been contracted for a long time), the ability to move in and out of many different perspectives is an even greater freedom. Walls are only a problem when you don't know where the door is and therefore can't get in or out.

True freedom is when you can move in and out of identification with a small sense of your self. You don't have to take my word for it. Find out what happens in your heart if you just let the opening and closing of your sense of self be just the way it is right now. Does this allow your heart to open? Does it allow you to just be for a moment?

Who Are You?

What is this Being that you are always sensing to some degree? Perhaps the most surprising discovery is that the sense of your self is not showing you anything about your true nature. A limited sense of your self is never about who you really are! It's not indicative of who you are but, rather, shows you how true your conditioning is. Recognizing this can turn your world inside out. The sense of your self is being shaped and limited by the unfolding of conditioned beliefs and ideas; it's not a reflection of your true nature.

This can be a tremendous relief. All of your experiences of limitation, incompleteness, contraction, insufficiency, or unworthiness have nothing to do with you! Instead, they are accurate reflections of the limitations, incompleteness, smallness, insufficiency, and unworthiness of your ideas, judgments, beliefs, concepts, fears, doubts, worries, hopes, dreams, and desires. They have nothing to do with the nature of you.

The most intimate experience of your self—your heart—is never a complete experience of your true self. It is always a relative experience of the functioning of that true self as it determines the relative degree of truth in the particular content of your experience.

This brings us back to the question: Who or what is the Being that you are always sensing to a greater or lesser degree? This question points to what is completely beyond words—and even beyond experience. Even the most expanded experience of Being is still not free of this shaping or limitation. In this case the question itself points to a bigger truth than any answer, even an experiential one.

What happens in your heart when you simply hold the question, Who am I or what am I? Even if your heart is open, you can still wonder who or what is experiencing the openness. The ultimate truth will never be captured in an experience because it's simply too big to fit in even the most expanded experience. This provides a clue to the question, Who are you? The reason an expanded sense of your self never quite contains the whole truth of your Being is that you are everything that exists.

Perhaps you can rest now from the dream of experiencing the ultimate truth. The truth is not dependent in any way on your experience of it. It is and always has been functioning just fine through what you call your experience of a self, without ever being contained in that experience. The sense of your self, whether it is expanded or contracted, is a functioning expression of a much larger Being that can never be fully captured in experience.

Perhaps the experience of truth doesn't need to be captured. Truth is something we can also unfold gradually bit by bit like a meal or novel that we slowly savor rather than rush through. We are and always have been realizing the truth even when we experience only a small part of it. The richness of Being is also revealed in the small truths that make up our lives.

Being is never harmed by the limited perspectives we experience. Being is not dependent on any particular way of sensing your self, nor even on the absence of a sense of self. Being is already resting within the endless opening and closing of your heart, so you might as well enjoy the ride.

> the truth catches up with me
> I am not enough
> never have been
> never will be
> what relief to admit this finite container
> can never contain infinity
> what joy to find infinity
> needs no container

Appendix 2: Love Is for Giving

The following is from Living from the Heart *by Nirmala, which is available at http://endless-satsang.com/free*

Love Is for Giving, Not for Getting

What is love and where is it found? We search for love and try to get love, and yet it seems like we never get enough. Even when we've found it, it can slip away as time passes. What if there is a source of love that never fades and is always available? What if love is as near and easy as breathing? What if you have been "looking for love in all the wrong places" instead of actually lacking love?

Love is both simpler and more mysterious and subtle than we imagine it to be. Love is simply the spacious, open attention of our awareness, which is the gentlest, kindest, and most intimate force in the world. It touches things without impinging on them. It holds all of our experience but doesn't hold it down or hold it back. And yet, inherent in awareness is a pull to connect and even merge with the object of your awareness.

It's this seemingly contradictory nature of awareness — the completely open and allowing nature of it and its passionate pull to blend with and even become the object of its attention — that gives life its depth and sweetness. There is nothing more satisfying than this delicious dilemma of being both apart from and, at the same time, connected to something you see, hear, or feel.

Awareness is the beginning of all separation. Prior to awareness, there is just oneness or "is-ness," with nothing separate from the oneness that would be able to experience it. With the birth of awareness comes the subtle distinction of two things: that which is aware and the object of awareness. And yet, those two are connected by this mysterious force we are calling awareness, or love.

This flow of awareness and love that connects you to all you experience is the true source of satisfaction and joy. We have all experienced it to some degree. Whenever you fall in love with a person, pet, piece of music, beautiful object, or anything else, you have felt this flow of intimate, connected awareness. Unfortunately, we've been taught to believe that the source of this good feeling was the object of our affection. So we suffered whenever we lost our apparent source. When your lover leaves, your beloved pet dies, the concert ends, or your dream home is repossessed, you feel bereft of that loving, connected feeling.

You Are the Source

But what if you are the source of the awareness that connects you to everything? What if the love you have been seeking has always been right here inside your own heart? What if it doesn't matter what your awareness touches, but only that awareness is flowing? That would profoundly simplify the search for love. Anything or any experience would be a suitable object for your love.

The sweetness of love is in the flow of awareness itself. The completely allowing openness and freedom you might look for from a perfect lover is already here in your own awareness. It doesn't have to try to be accepting because awareness is, by nature, open and allowing. By itself, awareness can't do anything but touch. It can't push or pull or demand something from or limit the freedom of what it touches. And yet, it is not an aloof, distant observer. It is deeply and intimately connected to the object of awareness. In fact, awareness and the object of awareness come from the same source and are ultimately the same thing.

This connection and intimacy that is natural in awareness is satisfying and fulfilling regardless of the object of awareness. In other words, whatever you are experiencing right now is your true love. Whatever you are experiencing is an opportunity to also experience the depth of your true nature as open, loving awareness. Your true nature is true love. It is the perfect lover you have been seeking, and not only is it always here, but it is who you really are.

You might be thinking, "But wait, I don't feel like I'm in love or loving all the time. Sometimes I feel lonely or angry and cut off from love and satisfaction." So how can it be that love is here, but you don't feel it? Is love really absent in those moments, or is it just limited in its expression and flow? Are there really moments when there is no awareness? Or is there always some awareness, even if it isn't a lot? If there were no awareness, there also would be no problems because awareness is the beginning of separation (the sense of a separate self), and the end of awareness is the end of separation. Practically speaking, without awareness, there can't be loneliness, anger, or anything else. So when you are lonely or angry, there is at least some awareness, although possibly not much.

Even when awareness is contracted and tight, as it often is when you are lonely, angry, sad, hurt, or afraid, it has the same nature as when you are happy and excited. Even a single drop of water is still wet, and even a single drop of awareness is still open and allowing of whatever it is touching.

The only trick to experiencing the open and allowing nature of awareness is to look for it in the actual experience you are having. When your awareness is contracted by judgment or fear, it's not actually touching the object of your judgment or fear. Instead, it is touching the judgmental or fearful thought you are having. Awareness is completely allowing and open to that thought. That is the definition of awareness: it is the open and allowing recognition of the content of our experience. If awareness is not open to something, then we are not aware of it.

The key to experiencing love is to notice where awareness is flowing right now. That flow of awareness is love, and it's the most satisfying and nourishing thing you can experience. There is naturally a direction to this flow of awareness. It moves from within your being to the objects nearby and the experiences you are having. You can only fully experience this flow of aware love as it moves in that direction.

When someone else is lovingly aware of you (not of their judgments or desires regarding you, but simply of you as you are), you can experience the outer expression of their love. You can see the way they are looking at you, the smile on their face, and their reactions to you. But the awareness of you is arising in them. The love is flowing from them toward you, and so it is filling them with a sense of satisfaction and joy. If you also are to feel satisfaction and joy, it will depend on whether you are experiencing a flow of love toward them. It is your own open awareness that fills you with that sense of connection and appreciation. You are filled with love when you are giving it to someone or something else.

Obviously, it's easier to open your heart and express love when the requirements of your conditioning are being met. When someone who matches your ideal for a lover is attracted to and interested in you, it's especially easy to give him or her the same openness and attention in return. So naturally, when two people are falling in love, they are both feeling the fullness and richness of the free flow of awareness, or love. But the contact each of them has with that love is within themselves. It's their own love and awareness that is filling them up so richly.

This truth—that you are filled with love when you love, rather than when you are loved—can free you from the search for love outside yourself. If you still aren't sure that it is your own love that fills you, think of a time when someone was in love with you, but you weren't in love with him or her. The flow of loving attention toward you wasn't satisfying. In fact, it might have been uncomfortable having someone so interested in you when you weren't feeling the same way.

In contrast, when you are falling in love with someone, it can be rich, exciting, and energizing, even if it isn't reciprocated. In unrequited love, there is an intensity and beauty from the outward flow of love that is filling you in that moment. So despite the disappointment and hurt of not being loved back, you experience a fullness and aliveness as a result of loving the other. In the Renaissance, unrequited love was even seen as an ideal. It's the love flowing out from your own heart that fills you with joy and satisfaction. The source is within you.

Just One Being

There is just one awareness and one Being behind all the individual awarenesses. The way you can reach that oneness of Being is by experiencing the flow of love from within your being. Paradoxically, the place where you are connected to others is inside your own heart. You can't really connect to another externally. Even if you used super glue to attach yourself to another person, there would still be a sense of separation in your outer experience, not to mention how hard it might be to disconnect!

On the inside, you are already connected to everyone and everything. The connection is this flow of awareness that is here right now reading these words. It is in the loving nature of awareness that the sense of connection is found, not in the objects of awareness. You are connected to others in the awareness flowing from within you to them. Connection is not found in the flow of awareness and love toward you, as that flow is connected to its source inside the other person.

This is good news! You can experience limitless love no matter what anyone else is doing. The only thing that matters is how much you are loving, not how much you are loved. Right now, you can be filled to overflowing with the incredible sweetness of love, just by giving awareness to anything and everything that is present in your experience. Don't take my word for it; test it out with this exercise:

Exercise: Allow your awareness to settle on a physical object nearby. Take an extra moment to allow your awareness to fully touch the object. Just for the sake of this experiment, give as much love, appreciation, and acceptance as you can to that object. Then notice another object. As your awareness rests for a moment on that, give it as much love, appreciation, and acceptance as you can.

Now allow your awareness to notice a sound in your environment. As you listen, give that same loving appreciation to the sound you are hearing.

If you have any difficulty giving love and appreciation to a particular object or sound, try another object or sound. If you pick a more neutral object or sound, it will be easier at first to experience loving something for no particular reason.

Continue allowing your awareness to land on various objects, sounds, colors, tastes, smells, and sensations. With each one, allow as much love and appreciation to flow toward it as you can. Take as long as you like with each experience, and if it's difficult to feel love toward something, just move on. It will get easier to love for no reason as you repeat this exercise.

Now notice other things that may be arising within you: an uncomfortable sensation, a thought, a feeling, or a desire. Take an extra moment to send loving attention toward it. Just for now, you can love each sensation, thought, feeling, or desire that appears within you.

As you get the hang of this, you can just allow your awareness to move naturally to whatever it touches next, either inside or outside of you. Whatever it lands on, give it love and acceptance. Just for a moment, let it be the way it is.

What is it like to give simple awareness and love over and over to things that appear in your experience? How open and full does your heart feel when you are able to give love in this way? If you come to something that's difficult to love or accept, just notice that it's difficult, and then love that it's difficult right now. You can even take a moment to simply love the way some things are harder to love than others. Then move on to whatever is in awareness next.

Just go ahead and love whatever is in front of you, and in that way be filled with love. It's that simple, if you remember that the essence of love is awareness and space. The ideal lover is someone who gives you lots of space to just be yourself but still connects with you as you are. Awareness is like that. It doesn't limit the object of its awareness, but it makes contact.

You Can't Run out of Love

You can give this awareness or love freely because awareness is the one thing you can never run out of. No matter how many things you've been aware of today, you still have awareness left for this moment and the next. Awareness is easy to give, and it doesn't cost anything or deplete you in any way. In your heart, there is a limitless supply of love. Just see if you can give so much attention to something that you end up with no more awareness.

We sometimes withhold love and awareness because we think that true love requires more than this simple, open attention. Our conditioning suggests that love requires things like compromise, sacrifice, and unconditional giving of our time and effort. Perhaps some of these are necessary for a relationship, but not for love.

This is an important distinction, as we often confuse love and relationship. We mistakenly believe that love is dependent on relationship. But if we recognize that the source of love is within us, then relationship can be seen in perspective. Relationships are important, but they aren't as important as love. The experience of this inner flow of love is satisfying, either with or without a relationship. You can experience it with a beautiful object of art in a museum, a moving piece of music, an exciting moment in a sporting activity, or in a deep connection with another person. Love is what makes relationships and everything else worthwhile.

What a rich possibility — that all the love you have ever wanted is available right now, just by giving it to everything you encounter, both within you and in the environment. Love is for giving, not for getting. And the more you give, the more fully it fills your heart to overflowing.

Loving Through the Senses

We are filled with love when we give it away, not when we receive it from others. This truth can profoundly free you from the search for love, as anything is a worthy object of your love. Especially when you realize that love is simply awareness and space, you can freely give it to everything that appears in your experience. In this way, you are filled to overflowing with the sweet open presence of love.

It is also possible to experience this fullness of love through your physical senses. For the most part, we use our senses to take things in: We look at something to get something, such as information. We might look in our wallet to see how much money we have left. Or we look in the fridge to see what there is to eat. We listen to the radio for some entertainment or news. We feel our pocket to see if our car keys are in there.

Or we might try to get something more than information through our senses: We watch carefully to try to feel safe. We stare longingly at a photo of someone to try to be filled with love or to be satisfied by their beauty. We listen to music to try to be filled with excitement or joy. In a sense we have learned to be consumers with our senses. We try to acquire beauty, pleasure, excitement, passion, happiness, security, value and even love by ingesting these through our senses. But just as love from the outside doesn't ever fill us up or completely satisfy us, anything we try to consume with our senses isn't ultimately satisfying.

Unfortunately, the experiences we take in through our senses do satisfy a little. Looking at a beautiful woman or man does give us a little bit of pleasure, excitement, and the experience of beauty. However, such pleasure and excitement are very fleeting and never enough. This is actually an unavoidable part of the nature of life and of our Being. The truth of our Being is pure emptiness or space. So when we take in any experience, it flows into the inner emptiness of our Being and, in the process, is dissolved by that emptiness. The inward flow of experience is a flow from form to emptiness. Everything we consume with our senses and awareness returns to its original nature as formless presence.

This is why the satisfaction we get from outer experience is never enough. Trying to fill ourselves up with beauty, passion, happiness, and love from the outside is like trying to fill a leaky bucket. No matter how long you stand there with the hose pouring water into that bucket, it never fills up. No matter how many experiences of passion, beauty, and joy you consume, the inner emptiness of your Being is still totally empty. And no matter how much love or attention you receive from others, it's never enough to fill the hole in your heart. You can never get enough of what doesn't satisfy.

Because of this, our attempts to feel good by ingesting or consuming outer experiences can lead to a compulsive or an addictive attachment to outer experiences, including fun, beauty, or romance. A basic principle of psychology is that an intermittent reward is more powerfully reinforcing than a constant one. So the little taste of excitement or satisfaction we do experience from seeing a beautiful person, tasting chocolate, or traveling to Fiji can lead to a slight, or even severe, addiction to the outer experience. People can become addicted to just about anything, including scanning the crowd for a beautiful face or planning ways to maximize fun or pleasure. This can also result in avoidance of or overreaction to things we don't want to experience: We may tighten or withdraw when we see the wrinkles in our lover's face, or we may not eat the healthiest foods if we don't want to taste them.

Fortunately, there is a simple solution. It is in the outward flow of the positive qualities of our Being, including love, that we can fully experience the peace, joy, love, and beauty within us. When joy, peace, or excitement is flowing from within us, it is moving from emptiness to form. The inner emptiness of Being is the source of everything, including joy, passion, peace, strength, compassion, support, and love. So it is in the outward flow of awareness and love that we are filled with the experience of these qualities. It's in this movement from emptiness to form that these particular qualities take shape. Emptiness moves into the particular forms of love, peace, joy, and everything else with the outward flow of awareness. Surprisingly, the inner empty source never runs out. There's always more joy and love to be found in their true source.

Because of the habit of trying to consume things with our senses, instead of feeling this fullness of Being, we often feel empty, hungry, and incomplete. So we go looking, listening, and feeling for something else to satisfy us. We may compulsively look for a better lover, a better car, or a better job even when the lover, car, or job we have is actually quite wonderful. We may develop the habit in the way we watch or listen to the world of always looking for something to take in with our senses that will satisfy us. Of course, many people experience this when it comes to food. We want joy and satisfaction by tasting something, and yet we can never eat enough. Similarly, we want joy and satisfaction from seeing or hearing something of beauty, but we can never see or hear enough to satisfy. Audiophiles are forever searching for a better sounding set of speakers.

There is another way: We can give love through our senses. Instead of trying to see or take in something exciting or satisfying with our eyes, we can shower whatever is in our sight with a flow of love through our eyes. This is as easy as shifting the focus to the outward flow of awareness rather than the inward flow of sensation.

Exercise: Take a moment to look at something in your environment. Start with something neutral or something you find pleasing to the eye. Notice how you are relating inwardly to the experience of sight. Are you trying to get something from looking? Is there an evaluation of what you are looking at? Is it good enough? Is it satisfying enough right now to simply look at this object?

Now allow a fuller flow of awareness through your eyes to the object. Instead of trying to take in the object through your eyes, shower it with a fullness of loving attention through your eyes.

Just for a moment, love it for no reason with your seeing. Love is acceptance and attention, so just give the object lots of attention and acceptance. Notice if you can feel a sense of love flowing out of your eyes to the object. Use your sight to give love to the object instead of to get something from it.

What is that like to feel an outward flow of love through your eyes? Don't worry if you are doing it right or if you are feeling it enough. Just notice how it shifts your experience to whatever degree it does, or just imagine a flow of love through your sense of sight to the object.

Now pick another object and, once again, allow loving awareness to flow out of your eyes to the object. Just for now, allow as much love as you can to flow through seeing to the object. Now move from object to object and shower each of them with love, just for the sake of this experiment. As you get the hang of it, you can even try it with objects you don't like or even strongly dislike. You can also try it with people and pets. Notice how some things are easier to look at this way than others, but give as much love to each thing as you can.

You can repeat this experiment with your other senses. What would it be like to shower things with love through your hearing? Your sense of touch? Your taste buds? What if the most important thing isn't how good your food tastes, but how much you love it with your mouth? We started with the sense of sight, as that sense has the greatest quality of separation or distance to it. Hearing, touch, and taste are just naturally more intimate senses, while seeing entails more of an experience of separation. However, that sense of separation can be profoundly shifted to a feeling of connectedness by giving love to things through your eyes. Here is a similar exercise for the sense of touch.

Exercise: Take a moment to touch something with your hands. Start with something neutral or something you find pleasing to touch, like a soft pillow or blanket. Notice how you are relating inwardly to the experience of touching. Are you trying to get something from the sensations in your hands? Is it satisfying enough to simply touch this object? Notice the inherent intimacy in touching something. There's no distance between you and the object you are touching. Is there really any separation right now as you touch it?

Now allow a fuller outward flow of awareness through your hands to the object. Instead of trying to take in the feel of the object, shower it with a fullness of loving attention through your hands. Just for a moment, love it for no reason with your touch. Love is ultimately acceptance and attention, so just give the object lots of attention and acceptance. Notice if you can feel a sense of love and acceptance flowing out of your hands to the object. Use your hands and the sense of touch to give love to the object instead of to get something from it.

How is it to feel an outward flow of love through your hands? Don't worry if you are doing it right or if you are feeling it enough. Just notice how it shifts your experience to whatever degree it does that, or just imagine a flow of love through your sense of touch to the object.

Now touch another object and, once again, allow loving awareness to flow out of your hands to the object. Just for now, allow as much love as you can to flow through your hands to the object. Now move from object to object and shower each of them with love, just for the sake of this experiment. As you get the hang of it, you can try this with objects you don't like to touch or even strongly dislike. You can also try it with people and pets. Notice how some things are easier to touch this way than others, but give as much love to each thing as you can.

Now include the internal sensations of your own body. In a very intimate way, you are touching everything inside of you. Your kinesthetic sense of touch includes being able to feel the joints, muscles, and even the organs of your body. Notice what happens if you give loving acceptance and attention to your arms and legs in the same way you did to the physical objects around you. Just for now, fully feel any sensation that arises in your body and directly send love and awareness to it.

Repeat the above exercise and substitute the sensation of hearing. Explore the experience of loving things through your ears. And then try it with the sense of smell and taste at your next snack or meal. Because these other senses are more intimate than the sense of sight, you may discover that it is very satisfying and rich to give love in these more immediate and intimate ways. You can also combine all your physical senses and love the totality of your present moment sensory experience:

Exercise: Take a moment to love something through one of your senses. Notice if you are trying to get something from the sensation. Now allow a fuller outward flow of awareness through your sensing to the object. Shower the object with a fullness of loving attention. Just for a moment, love it for no reason.

Now notice another sensation and allow love and acceptance to flow to another sight, sound, smell, taste, or tactile sensation. And then love another sensation and another and so on. Be sure to include the sensations of your own body, including whatever is happening inside of you and whatever you can experience of your own body through sight, listening, and touch.

How is it to feel an outward flow of love through all your senses? Don't worry if you are doing it right or if you are feeling it enough. Just notice how it shifts your experience to whatever degree it does, or just imagine a flow of love through all of your senses to your present moment experiences.

Now allow awareness and spaciousness to flow to all your sensory experience at once. Include every sensation you are having, and notice that you can love them all at the same time. The source of awareness is limitless, and you can't run out of awareness and love, so why not give as much awareness and love as you can to everything that's here right now? Don't worry if you are including everything or not. Just allow your awareness to flow out in as many directions and to as many sensations as you can. What is it like to just love the totality of your sensations?

Loving Beyond the Senses

You can include more subtle sensations if you experience these, but being able to experience subtle energies and dimensions isn't necessary to experiencing the fullness of love. Thoughts, emotions, and desires are also a more subtle level of experience than physical sensations.

Exercise: Take a moment to love something through one of your senses. Now allow a fuller outward flow of awareness through your sensing to the object. Shower it with a fullness of loving attention. Notice another sensation and allow love and acceptance to flow to another sight, sound, smell, taste, or tactile sensation. Then love another sensation and another and so on. Allow awareness and spaciousness to flow out of all your senses at once. Include every physical sensation you are having, and notice that you can love them all at the same time.

Now notice any thoughts or emotions that are arising, and allow this same loving attention to flow to them as well. If a strong desire or longing arises, include it in the total flow of open awareness. And if you sense any energy or presence in the room, love it for no reason as well. Don't be concerned if you don't sense anything beyond the physical, as it really doesn't matter. Just love whatever you are experiencing in this moment. It is satisfying to love anything and everything, so why leave anything that is here right now out of this abundant flow of sensing and awareness? What is it like to include everything in your loving flow of awareness?

You can even love whatever you are not experiencing in this moment. You can love through your physical senses, through pure awareness, and through sensing existence itself. In this way, you can love the entire universe and beyond. It is rich to love what's here in your direct experience, and you can also simultaneously love what lies beyond your immediate sensory experience. Just send love to everything even if you can't see it or feel it. What is it like to simply give more and more love?

There is one more place you can send love, and that is to all time:

Exercise: Love whatever you are experiencing in this moment. Include everything in your loving flow of awareness: everything you can see, hear, touch, feel, and everything you can't. Let love flow to the infinite reaches of space throughout the universe and beyond.

You can also send love through this present moment in time to every other moment in time. Start by loving the exquisite immediacy of the experience you are having in this moment, and then send love to every memory or thought about the future that arises in the immediacy of this present moment. Now also send love to the past and future, to the endless array of intensely immediate "nows" that have ever appeared and that will ever appear. Don't worry if you are doing it right. Just send love, and let the love find its own way to the past and future. Notice what it's like to love the entire flow of time. Include as much of eternity as you can.

Notice what your experience of the present moment is like when you allow limitless love and acceptance to flow out of this moment to every other moment in time. Does loving all the moments of your life and beyond limit or restrict your experience of this moment? Or does loving all of time allow you to even more fully experience and love the precious uniqueness of this very instant? Paradoxically, loving all time can bring us into even more intimate contact with the present moment.

You don't need to pick and choose what to love. Anything will do, from a dryness in your mouth, to the feel of a dog's fur, to the sound of the wind, to the mystery of thought, to the infinity of space itself, or even to a direct mystical sensing of something beyond your normal senses, such as the infinite expanse of time itself.

The wonderful thing about being filled with love and joy from showering simple awareness and love on whatever appears in our experience is that it frees us from having to find or get the right experiences or from having to avoid the wrong ones. If you can be filled to overflowing with the sweetness of love by looking at a plastic wastebasket in this way, consider how that might affect your Saturday night dates! While you don't have to marry the first person you shower with love through your eyes, you may discover that physical appearance isn't as important to love and romance as you thought. Similarly, it might not matter as much as you thought what song is playing on the radio, what is being served for dinner, whether you are having an expanded or contracted experience, whether you are suffering or not, or what is happening period. If everything is a potential object for this limitless flow of love, then you can just relax and love whatever is in front of you or whatever is happening right now.

Love Reveals Inner Beauty

There is an even more surprising discovery you may make: When you shower something with love, it reveals its inner beauty. Just as a black light reveals the fluorescence in a poster from the sixties, the love in your awareness can reveal the beauty, value, wonder, and intrinsic worth and perfection that is in everything. The secret to experiencing more perfection in the world isn't to create a flawless life full of exquisite objects of art, beautiful lovers, delicious food, and exclusively pleasurable experiences, but to shower every object, every person, and every experience with the inner fullness of love until its inner beauty shines with a profound radiance. You can do this in a fantastic mansion or at the local garbage dump. You can do this with a beautiful movie star or with the grouchy old man who lives on your street.

You can also do this with your own body and personality. This love that flows through your senses is actually what you are. The body and personality that you experience yourself as are really just more objects to love. All the reactions, thoughts, desires, and inner sensations that arise within you are simply more things to love. They are as beautiful as everything else.

There is also intense and vast beauty, perfection, and wonder within the larger dimensions of your Being. Empty space reveals a glorious texture, fullness, and softness beyond the softest thing in the universe when you love it fully and without reservation. Time becomes an infinite playground of possibility and creation when you love it with all your heart. Presence and all the qualities of your being, including love, peace, joy, clarity, and strength are the most delicious flavors you can imagine when you just love them with all your senses and with awareness itself.

Don't take my word for any of this. Find out for yourself what happens when you love for no reason, especially if you include anything and everything. Love is for giving and giving, and then giving some more.

Beyond the Experience of Love

Beyond the possibility of experiencing more and more love in your heart, is the even richer discovery that love is what you are, and what you have always been. This open flow of awareness is what you are made of. It is your true nature. When you are experiencing more love, you are experiencing more of your true self.

The recognition that love is your essence, your nature, allows an ultimate sense of fullness that isn't dependent even on experiencing love. If love is what you are, then it doesn't matter if you are experiencing it right now or not. If for a moment you don't experience your shoulders, do you lose your shoulders? No, they are part of you and are always here, whether you are noticing them or not. This is not to say that it doesn't matter whether you experience the complete potential for love that exists within you. However, once you have discovered and repeatedly experienced the truly limitless nature of the love that you are, it doesn't matter whether you are experiencing that right now or not because you know that that infinite potential is still who you are and who you will always be.

While it's rich to explore and discover the limitless capacity of your heart to love, and then love some more, you can also simply rest here as love itself. Love at rest is still love. When love is resting as the pure potential for love, it is just another dimension of its accepting and allowing nature.

Love is not just a part of you; it's the nature, or essence, of every part of you. The capacity for open, spacious awareness is always here, even if you are using only a very small portion of this capacity. All of the exercises and prescriptions in this book are actually descriptions of what has always been true. No matter how much or how little love is flowing in this moment, love is still always here. It's who you are and who you have always been.

Every moment of your entire life has been an experience of the flow of awareness and love to something. Even when love isn't being experienced, there isn't any less love; there is just less of the outward flow or expression. The source is still here in all its glory. Love is not only for giving, it is what you are.

> I may think I feel love,
> but it is love that feels me,
> constantly testing the woven fibers
> that enclose and protect my heart
> with a searing flame
> that allows no illusion of separation.
>
> and as the insubstantial fabric of my inner fortress
> is peeled away by the persistent fire,
> I desperately try to save some charred remains

by escaping into one more dream of passion.
I may think I can find love,
but it is love that finds me.

meanwhile, love becomes patient and lies in wait,
its undying embers gently glowing,
and even if I now turn and grasp after the source of
warmth,
I end up cold and empty-handed.
I may think I can possess love,
but it is love that possesses me.

and finally, I am consumed,
for love has flared into an engulfing blaze
that takes everything
and gives nothing in return.
I may think love destroys me,
but it is love that sets me free.

ABOUT THE AUTHOR

After a lifetime of spiritual seeking, Nirmala met his teacher, Neelam, a devotee of H.W.L. Poonja (Papaji). Neelam convinced Nirmala that seeking wasn't necessary; and after experiencing a spiritual awakening in India, Nirmala began offering satsang with Neelam's blessing. This tradition of spiritual wisdom has been most profoundly disseminated by Ramana Maharshi, a revered Indian saint, who was Papaji's teacher. Nirmala's perspective has also been greatly expanded by his friend and teacher, Adyashanti.

Nirmala is also the author of *Nothing Personal, Living from the Heart, Meeting the Mystery, Gifts with No Giver, That Is That,* and other writings, which are available on his website: www.endless-satsang.com. Nirmala also offers Nondual Spiritual Mentoring sessions in person or over the phone. He lives in Sedona, Arizona with his wife, Gina Lake. More information about her and her books is available at radicalhappiness.com.

Nondual Spiritual Mentoring

Nondual Spiritual Mentoring with Nirmala is available to support you in giving attention and awareness to the more subtle and yet more satisfying inner dimensions of your being. Whether you have a single mentoring session or participate in ongoing one-to-one spiritual guidance, these sessions are an opportunity to more completely orient your life toward the true source of peace, joy, and happiness. Nirmala has worked with thousands of individuals and groups around the world to bring people into a direct experience of the truth of oneness beyond the illusion of separation. To arrange an appointment, please use the contact form at endless-satsang.com.

More Books by Nirmala

Links to purchase Nirmala's books or to download them as free pdf ebooks are here: http://endless-satsang.com/free

Living from the Heart

A free collection of teachings about the Heart, including:

Part One: *From the Heart: Dropping out of Your Mind and Into Your Being*: Offers simple ways to shift into a more open and accepting perspective and to experience your true nature as aware space.

Part Two: *The Heart's Wisdom*: Points the reader back to the Heart, the truest source of wisdom.

Part Three: *Love Is for Giving, Not for Getting*: Points to the true source of love in your own heart. It is by giving love that we are filled with love.

That Is That: Essays About True Nature

A collection of articles and answers to questions posed by spiritual seekers. It captures the essence of spiritual inquiry and provides the reader with a real transmission of Presence on every page. It is much more than an exposition about our true nature as infinite consciousness, it offers an experiential exploration of who we really are, not only through the transmission in the words, but through the many thoughtful questions it raises.

Meeting the Mystery: Exploring the Aware Presence at the Heart of All Life

What is the source of the aliveness and awareness, which are fundamental to all life? What is the nature of desire, and how do our desires relate to suffering? How do we know what is true? What is the nature of belief, and how do our beliefs affect our ability to experience the deeper reality that is always here? And in the midst of these mysteries, how do we live our daily lives in the most satisfying and integrated way? *Meeting the Mystery* explores these questions and will help you discover new dimensions and possibilities in your life.

Gifts with No Giver: A Love Affair with the Truth

A free collection of nondual spiritual poetry by Nirmala. Here is a sample poem:

every taste
every sensation
every possible pleasure
is already present
in the timeless
awareness
that is beating my heart
what use
in chasing dreams
that have already
come true

Nothing Personal: Seeing Beyond the Illusion of a Separate Self

In this concisely edited collection of satsang talks and dialogues, Nirmala "welcomes whatever arises within the field of experience. In the midst of this welcoming is always an invitation to inquire deeply within, to the core of who and what you are. Again and again, Nirmala points the questions back to the questioner and beyond to the very source of existence itself—to the faceless awareness that holds both the question and the questioner in a timeless embrace." –From the Foreword by Adyashanti.

Links to purchase Nirmala's books or to download them as free pdf ebooks are here: http://endless-satsang.com/free